The

NORMAL

CHRISTIAN CYCLE

Unlocking the Secret to the Fullness of Christ

BOLA OLU-JORDAN

The

NORMAL

CHRISTIAN CYCLE

Unlocking the Secret to the Fullness of Christ

BOLA OLU-JORDAN

A step-by-step discipleship manual for believers, showing the whole panorama of the plan, purpose and process of salvation

Africa. Canada. USA.

The Normal Christian Cycle

Unlocking the Secret to the Fullness of Christ

Copyright © Bola Olu-Jordan, 2015

All rights reserved.

This book is protected by copyright laws. This book may not be copied or reprinted for commercial gain or profit. The use of short quotations or occasional page copying for personal or group study is permitted and encouraged, provided there is no alteration and the source is duly acknowledged.

All scripture quotations, except otherwise specified are taken from the King James Version of the Bible, Public domain.

The Normal Christian Cycle and other CRYOUT Publishing books can be purchased in bulk by churches, ministries and other organizations for evangelical, educational or discipleship purposes. For information, please send your request via email to: info@cryoutpublishing.com

ISBN-13: 978-9785037746

Published by CRYOUTPublishing.com

Printed in the United States of America

DEDICATION

Matilda, Modupe, Momade, Mojoyin and Mofeoluwa

Contents

	Dedication	v
	Preface	xi
	Acknowledgments	xv
	Introduction	xvii
	SECTION 1	
1.	Another Gospel	1
2.	Good Intention	11
3.	Partnership	27
4.	The Cycle	49
5.	Dispensation of Rebellion	67
	SECTION II	
6.	Birth	87
7.	Basic Principles	117
8.	The Spirit Reality	149
9.	Life	167
10.	Abundant Life	191
	References	234

That Christ may dwell in your hearts by faith; that ye, being rooted and grounded in love, May be able to comprehend with all saints what is the breadth, and length, and depth, and height; And to know the love of Christ, which passeth knowledge, that ye might be filled with all the fullness of God
Ephesians 3: 1-19

Preface

"Christianity today is so subnormal that if any Christian began to act like a normal New Testament Christian, he would be considered abnormal."

THE ABOVE QUOTE was made several decades ago and credited to Leonard Ravenhill. Whatever he saw at that time that made him say those words was nothing compared to what is happening today in the Christendom.

The advent of hyper-Charismatic movement has undoubtedly brought about an upsurge in mega churches, and with it comes its mega problems. This movement has somewhat deregulated the Christian faith walk to the extent of conferring the *born again* title on more people than ever in history of the church, all in the name of unity, demonstration of the power of the Holy Spirit, and 'church growth.'

The representation of the infilling of the Holy Spirit by this group is a near scandalous display of emotions, excited utterances, spiritual ecstasy and demonstration of feelings. Worship services are colored with social appeal and the atmosphere energized by soul music with an eclectic orgy. It is crowned by the charming and affectionate 'pastor,' who is more of a motivational speaker than a Gospel preacher. He heats up the atmosphere with oratory words, emotionally charged healings and miracles, which are more of a placebo, and fades away as quickly as it comes. Alas! This is the Christianity many know. The explosion and societal appeal it has, especially on the youth is a confirmation of divine acceptance to them. Consequently, many have accepted as normal what is really abnormal.

How did the church degenerate from the level of apostolic fire and revival to spiritual lethargy and compromise? She has lost the fundamental apostolic principles, and therefore, no longer experience the fullness of Christ as it was in the early church. She no longer demonstrates the true presence and power of the Holy Spirit. Believers are now introduced to a faith walk of mere doctrines without power or power without the Holy Spirit. Either way, believers do not experience the genuine new birth, which is the core and the first step in the faith walk. Consequently, they cannot walk in the fullness of Christ as the early church did. If the foundation be destroyed, what can the righteous do? (Psa 11:3)

In the midst of this error, however, I have been blessed and encouraged by many Bible teachers, who strive to restore these fundamental doctrines with biblical and apostolic emphasis. Their works have answered many questions like: "when does the new birth really occur?" "Is it once and for all?" "Are we saved into the church or into Christ?" "Is the new birth the same as being born again?" "Are the gifts for us today?" And so on. But I still have a burden…

As a believer of over two decades with passion for discipleship, I'm still sad to see sincere believers run with just a part of the Christian faith walk, totally oblivious of the rest. These are similar to the believers in Ephesus (Act 19). They become frustrated when the fireworks they try to ignite with just a part of the truth end up like that of the sons of Sceva (Act 19:4). This confirms that half-truth is even more dangerous than a whole lie.

I long to see believers walk in not just a part but the whole apostolic principles necessary for a normal Christian. Only this can restore the church and can make believers experience the fullness of Christ and the manifestation of the power and presence of the Holy Spirit as the early believers did.

Upon this burden, this work is presented. It is my hope that believers will be able to discover some of these principles by the revelation of the Holy Spirit as they read this book. They are the secrets that made the early church walk in such power and anointing that they were said to have "turned the world upside down." (Act 17:6) If a part of the experience of Christ is the glory that the Church manifests in the world today, imagine what the fullness will be.

We must see from God's point of view and not from the traditional church's point of view. God is not a God of movement or organization. He did not give us a system, religion or denomination; He did not even give us Christianity: He gave us a Person, Christ Jesus. It is Him alone that can reveal these truths to us, if only we are humble enough to do away with what we already know and let His Spirit reveal His mind to us. Religious knowledge is always a deterrent to spiritual revelation.

May you be blessed reading!

'Bola Olu-Jordan, Sunny Isles Beach, Florida, September 21, 2014.

Acknowledgments

I GIVE THANKS to God for rescuing this book from the fate of its peers who are still *imprisoned* and waiting for a day of liberty like this. If God did it with this, He will do it with them.

I acknowledge the untiring labor of the following people, whose efforts in the defense of the true Gospel, walk of faith, friendship, fellowship and relationship have greatly influenced my faith walk with Jesus, and also this publication: Gordon Gentry, David Sheats, whose love to see believers seeing not only a part but the fullness of Christ introduced me to the works of David Pawson. Pawson's works, particularly book, the Normal Christian Birth is part of the springboard in which the foundation of this work is presented. I also acknowledge Dr. Bern Zumpano, whose life and works are the introduction to the deep things of God and walking in power in my life.

I acknowledge the precious time of fellowship, sharing, teaching and discipleship in West Palm Beach, Miami, Maryland, Ghana, Kenya and particularly Nigeria. The "precept upon precept; line upon line, here a little, there a little" have all pieced together to make the whole.

Last but not the least, the efforts of Dr. Jon Osamor, brother Femi Ajayi and others, without whose support this book would not have been published.

Introduction

THIS BOOK CAME into being from a series of teachings and discipleship classes with various local gatherings.

In one of such meetings, a two-day believers' retreat held in Ibadan, Nigeria in April 2014 with the theme, *Unveiling the Mysteries of the Ages, from Eden to Millennium,* a brother, mystified by the revelation of who a Christian and the church truly are asked a heart-probing question. It was similar to the questionPeter asked when Jesus made a remarkable statement about riches, sequel to the rich young ruler's inability to fulfill Jesus' instruction to him about eternal life.

Jesus had earlier responded to the rich young ruler's question by telling him to go and keep the laws, but he seemed to think that was too simple because he had been doing that from his youth; he wanted something more. Jesus then told him to go and sell all he had, give the proceeds to the poor, and come follow Him, it was one instruction too many for him. He went away sorrowfully, because "he had great possession." Then Jesus said to the disciples: "Verily I say unto you, that a rich man shall hardly enter into the kingdom of heaven. And again I say unto you, it is easier for a camel to go through the eye of a needle, than for a rich man to enter into the kingdom of God." (Mat 19:16-24)

The disciples were mystified about Jesus' somewhat *radical* conclusion about riches. They could not reconcile or understand why Jesus raised such a bar for rich people to make heaven. They were "exceedingly amazed and asked: "who then can be saved?" (vs 19:25).

In the same vein, when the revelation and the truth of what the church really is, and consequently who a Christian is dawned on this brother, he asked this question: "what then, is the church, and who then, is a Christian?"

From experience, until believers get to this junction where our theology is torched by the truth in order to reveal the dross, and we stand face to face with the revelation of God that challenges our dear doctrines and shakes the very foundation of our beliefs, we cannot ask such questions. And until we ask such questions, we are not yet seeing by the Spirit the whole panorama of the plan and purpose of God for the church.

When the reality of Jesus and the truth of God dawns on us, it destroys the fabric of our religious mindset and removes self-direction, except to turn to God and ask such questions: "who then can be saved?" "Who are You, Lord?" "Who is a true Christian?" It is until then that God can reveal the truth to us. Such truths, more often than not, may negate our beliefs and impossible to fulfill. That is when the answer of Jesus to the disciples becomes relevant: *"with man it is impossible, but with God all things are possible."* (Mat 19:26).

Moses and Paul are examples of those who got their theology shaken with an encounter with God, and they too, asked such questions. If you are at this junction in your Christian life, and you seem to have more questions than answers, and it appears no one is giving the answer that resonates with the Spirit of God in you, God will surely reveal Himself to you. His revelation will probably blow you away like he did to the disciples. This is because it may tamper with, challenge or deflate your erstwhile belief and theology as he did to the rich ruler, and the disciples.

This book is therefore written to believers who are at the junction of God's revelation and asking many similar questions which seem to challenge their own very belief. Also to those who are finding it difficult to reconcile the revelation of God in their hearts with the theology and doctrines they have learned or faced. You have to come to the understanding that the things of the spirit are spirits. They look foolish to man, we can only understand them by His Spirit, and they are "yea and amen."

The answer of Jesus was more to correct the rich man's attitude towards riches than to judge him. It was as shocking to the ruler who could not follow Jesus as well as the disciples who were already following Him. An encounter with Jesus is always a shocking process; it shakes the core of our belief.

The basic lesson this should teach us is that we should come to Jesus without a preconceived mindset or idea of what we already know or think is right. Jesus is also calling believers today to do exactly what He called the rich man to do, the platform might be a little different. However, our response must not be like that of the rich man, but of the disciples: "lo, we have left all and we follow you." (Luk 18:28)

Successive movements have introduced us to a service of fulfilling more than that of following. Following Jesus with the simple heart of a fisherman is better than fulfilling all the laws from our youth like the rich young ruler.

One of the challenges of denominations is that they all run with the part they know and holding it as the absolute. Many even build doctrines or empires around it. For instance, while the Pentecostal emphasizes more of the power of God at Pentecost, especially speaking in tongues as the evidence of the baptism of the Holy Spirit, the Charismatic is more about the demonstration of the gifts of the spirit, which many do with so much abandon as to raise a bar over its validity.

The truth is that we need to comprehend the whole plan of God, not just a part. We must also understand that God is not a God of any movement or denomination, but of truth and love. It is important to emphasize the truth, even when it challenges our doctrines. We cannot sacrifice the truth on the altar of unity and vice versa. They are like a Siamese twin. He is the God of love, and we must present the love of God in love and in truth. This is what this book seeks to present.

This book is divided into two sections. The first is a precursor to the second. It is a developmental plot, so it is best followed in order. If you attempt to jump to a topic that interests you without following through, you may end up running with half-truth or false conclusion. Some thoughts are plotted in a chapter, but conclusions are in subsequent chapters. So, do not form conclusion on things until you read through without denominational bias, carry-over mentality or doctrinal bottle-neck.

It must be stated that there are many truths we will only understand by and by, but as believers living in the tail end of the last days, the words of the scripture must come to pass right before our eyes: all mysteries shall be finished as God reveals them to His servants, the prophets. (Rev 10:7)

Here are some basic foundational Christian truths, some of which have disappeared from many pulpits today. It is, however, important for a believer to know these truths to be able to enter into a normal Christian cycle that begins with birth and culminates at eternal life.

Please, Come along!

SECTION 1

*For we are made partakers of Christ,
if we hold the beginning of our
confidence stedfast
unto the end.*
Hebrews 3:14

1

ANOTHER GOSPEL

For if he that cometh preacheth another Jesus, whom we have not preached, or if ye receive another spirit, which ye have not received, or another gospel, which ye have not accepted, ye might well bear with him.
- 2 Corinthians 11:4

THE TITLE, THE Normal Christian Cycle presupposes that there is an abnormal Christian cycle. While that doesn't sound right, spiritually (if it is "abnormal," then, it is not a cycle at all), but this book is presented in the context of what many have grown to know as Christianity today, which, as you will find out is not the Christianity of Jesus.

If the early apostles or the "cloud of witnesses" had the opportunity to take a peep into the 'Christianity' of today, words like "strange," "odd" and "bizarre" might trail behind "abnormal." To us, however, everything seems normal.

The Christian life is a cycle of experience in God through Jesus by the Holy Spirit in a believer's life. (Heb 6:1-2, Col

2:6-8) But there is another cycle that looks just like it: it is experienced through denominations and Christian activities (Gal 1:6-9). It introduces believers to a strange gospel and a different cycle

This is similar to the two churches: one being built by Jesus (Mat 16:18), which is invisible, cannot be founded, headed by men or joined, and membership is by spiritual birth; it is the true church, and the other being built by [sincere] men, founded, headed, owned, and led by men through activities and doctrines, and membership is by joining; it is the organized church.

Many simply grow into Christianity without experiencing the spiritual birth, let alone other stages of Christian faith walk. Others rise through the religious ranks and become leaders. Thus, many Christian gatherings are founded on religious mindset and there are religious centers, loosely called church where these religions activities are carried out, whereas the true church cannot be seen because it is an expression.

As alarming as that may sound, however, there is comfort in the words of Jesus. He says that He will build His church, and the gate of hell will not prevail against it. (Mat 16:18) This is good news; that Jesus did not leave man to build His church for Him, just like God did not leave man to save himself (of course, he cannot). There are palpable evidences around us of what man can build for Jesus if he were to build His Church. That is the best man has ever done and will ever do, though with good intentions.

Today, Jesus is barely allowed in His church. The Holy Spirit is much talked about but less in control. Churches are more of a gathering of those with the innate desire to worship God their own way, but true Christianity is a personal relationship with a Person.

It is time to rediscover the apostolic principles of charting the normal course of Christ without the encumbrance of Christianity. The personal relationship with Christ is the firepower of the early church. It made early believers to experience not just a part but the fullness of Christ. Therefore, they were able to walk in unity -"one accord." This is one mighty weapon that the church has lost (Joh 17), and which sadly, Satan has turned into mere ecumenism. (Act 1:14, Mat 18:19)

Christ Lost to Christianity
The last day church has lost the fundamental apostolic principles which were the basis of the early church and the secret of believers' power. These principles have been replaced by doctrines, system has replaced a Person, mere desire and theological accent of studying Christ has replaced personal relationship, and religious programs have replaced the process of maturing in Christ. Christ is lost to Christianity, denominations replaced the one true Church and the apostolic leadership gave way to institutional oligarchy.

This scenario continued into many centuries. More truths and more secrets of the power of the church were lost. As the years pass by, the church metamorphosed more into a religious movement than a fellowship, a religion than a relationship with Jesus. It became more political than spiritual. Laws replaced the Holy Spirit, rationalism and intellectualism replaced revelation. By and by, the devil successfully returned the church to the same state he grounded Adam and Eve, and also Israel. He took them out of the will of God and made them choose their own path of getting back to God, neglecting God's ordained path, which He designed for man to get to Him.

The last day church is no doubt rich. But her riches are the benefits of Satan's generosity. Satan's strategy since the beginning of ages is to offer a beautiful apple: "good for food, "pleasant to the eyes," "to be desired to make one wise." Not only did he encourage Eve, who is the prophetic representation of the Church to eat, but also shared with her husband.

The church does not only pride herself in prostituting with Satan's generous offer, but she shares the cup of her abominations with her harlot offspring (the denominations) and also with the kings of the earth.

While God will return the first woman (Eve), the representation of the true church to "a glorious church, not having spot, or wrinkle, or any such thing; but that it should be holy and without blemish" (Eph 5:27), John, the beloved saw the revelation of the other woman:

> *And the woman was arrayed in purple and scarlet colour, and decked with gold and precious stones and pearls, having a golden cup in her hand full of*

> *abominations and filthiness of her fornication: And upon her forehead was a name written, MYSTERY, BABYLON THE GREAT, THE MOTHER OF HARLOTS AND ABOMINATIONS OF THE EARTH. And I saw the woman drunken with the blood of the saints, and with the blood of the martyrs of Jesus: and when I saw her, I wondered with great admiration. (Rev 17:4-6)*

No religion in history claims the martyrdom of the saints more than Christianity herself. Although, many like to put this blame solely on the doorstep of the then Catholic church, but true as that may be, her offspring continue the same disaster in a more subtle way, using different styles and strategies against the true church. They continue to make the "kings of the earth" and "inhabitants of the earth" drunk (brainwashed by the false gospel of materialism, miracles, etc.) and follow her (membership). Like mother, like daughter as the Bible rightly said about the harlot. She has fame, money, power and people. Many are innocent members of this counterfeit church.

Same Old Serpent

The devil hasn't changed much. Whether Satan offers an apple or dangles a carrot, they are full of worms. His tool is attraction and fascination. He tried it with Jesus when He was fasting in the wilderness, not for a day or two or just a few days but forty days. Satan is not afraid of the anointing; he rather goes where the anointing is. He has no reason to attack the church if she does not have the anointing. Isn't he more faithful and committed to his mission and ministry than an average Christian today? Even his children are, in their generation, wiser than the children of light (Luk 16:8). He is still busy walking to and fro, offering his benefits.

The Powerless Church
Although Adam and Eve fell to Satan in the Garden of Eden, Jesus overcame him in the Garden of Gethsemane. He then gave the church the power and the authority to do the same. The disciples demonstrated this power even before Jesus was crucified:

> *The seventy returned again with joy, saying, Lord, even the devils are subject unto us through thy name. And he said unto them, I beheld Satan as lightning fall from heaven. Behold, I give unto you power to tread on serpents and scorpions, and over all the power of the enemy: and nothing shall by any means hurt you. (Luk 10:17-19)*

After the cross, Jesus reinforced this authority to believers:

> *And these signs shall follow them that believe; In my name shall they cast out devils; they shall speak with new tongues; They shall take up serpents; and if they drink any deadly thing, it shall not hurt them; they shall lay hands on the sick, and they shall recover. (Mar 16:17-18)*

Jesus gave the church this authority and the early church used it and walked in it with astounding miracles and manifestations. From Peter at the Beautiful Gate, to Philip, Stephen, and even Paul, who claimed that he saw Jesus "last of all… as of one born out of due time." (1Co 15:8)

Why is the church no longer manifesting this power and authority? She has done it before, why is it that she can no longer do it again? What has changed: God, Jesus, Holy Spirit or the church? The answer is that the church has simply believed another Jesus, received another Spirit and believed another Gospel (2Co 11:4). This has weakened her hands. It has made her both prayerless, powerless and made her prey to the counterfeit church. The enemy has persuaded her away from the apostolic principles of Jesus. The writer of the book of Hebrew calls it "the elementary principles of the doctrines of Christ." (Heb 6:1-2) Truly elementary, but the church has lost it completely. It is the foundation of the church, the core of our faith. Except there is a foundational restoration, the church cannot return to her rightful position.

Does the church know this?

It is one and the same as asking if Adam and Eve knew that they had fallen. The answer is "yes." They realized that they could no longer have fellowship with God in the Garden as they used to in the cool of the day. When they heard the voice of God, it no longer brought them comfort but fear.

The Proud Church
Just like Adam and Eve tried to cover their nakedness when they discovered that they were naked in the Garden, so also the last day church. The difference, however between Adam and Eve and the last day church is that Adam and Eve

admitted their nakedness, and that was why they could get help from God. But the last day church does not know that she is not only naked, but "wretched, and miserable, and poor, and blind" (Rev 3:17), sadly, she does not realize it. How then can she get help?

In His mercy, God clothed Adam and Eve and rescued them from eternal death. He took them away from the Garden so that they would not eat from the tree of life and live forever in their fallen state, beyond redemption. But the last day church does not allow God to clothe her. She rather says, "I am rich, and increased with goods, and have need of nothing." (Rev 3:17). She says she does not need anything. Therefore, Jesus could not rescue her as God rescued Adam and Eve in the Garden. The best Jesus could do is this:

> *I counsel thee to buy of me gold tried in the fire, that thou mayest be rich; and white raiment, that thou mayest be clothed, and that the shame of thy nakedness do not appear; and anoint thine eyes with eyesalve, that thou mayest see. (Rev 3:18-19)*

She Can Rise

The path to repentance for the church is to know where she has fallen. She fell at the point of neglecting the apostolic principles of the doctrines of the church. That is the foundation of the church and the believer's map to walking with Christ. We cannot experience the fullness of Christ without fully coming to Him. We must return to our first love. We must not only return to the first principles of the doctrines of Christ but also follow it to the letter. This is the normal Christian cycle.

Buy this gold, tried in the fire, so that you will be rich and clothe yourself with the righteousness of Christ to cover the shame of your nakedness, and rescue your life from the hands of touts and rascals who have taken over the pulpit, peddling falsehood to innocent victims. Anoint your eyes with eye-salves so that you can see that without these principles, believers cannot experience all of Christ, and if we do not experience all of Him, we are none of Him.

This is the way God has made for man to come to Him, every other way are the ways of man: religion, Christianity, traditions and denominations. They are not God's way. The course of Christ must take the normal cycle He has made for man to come to Him. Our ways do not and cannot lead us to God. Jesus said:

> *As many as I love, I rebuke and chasten: be zealous therefore, and repent. Behold, I stand at the door, and knock: if any man hear my voice, and open the door, I will come in to him, and will sup with him, and he with me. (Rev 3:20)*

There is grace to save now, but soon, the mercy that brings the grace will end and it will turn into judgment. Let your faith rise to take the grace of God, which has appeared to us. (Tit 2:11; 3:4)

> *For many walk, of whom I have told you often, and now tell you even weeping, that they are the enemies of the cross of Christ... (Php 3:18)*

2

GOOD INTENTION

"And the LORD said unto David my father, Whereas it was in thine heart to build an house unto my name, thou didst well that it was in thine heart. Nevertheless thou shalt not build the house; but thy son that shall come forth out of thy loins, he shall build the house unto my name."
- 1 Kings 8:18-19

God's *Magic*

THE FALL OF man brought a total separation from God. Man died a spiritual death, just as God had warned. He was no longer able to communicate or commune with God, spirit to spirit as he used to in the cool of the day. But in His mercy, God still put a part of Himself in man. This was to enable him to hear God's voice once more, even in a fallen state, and so, Adam and Eve "heard the voice of the LORD God walking in the Garden in the cool of the day," although they hid themselves "from the presence of the LORD God amongst the trees of the garden. And the LORD God called unto Adam, and said unto him, where art thou?" (Gen 3:8-9)

This part of God, which He graciously put into man, is like a spark designed to guide man back home to God. Although he is fallen, he will not be lost forever. This spark is the connecting *magic* that God in His infinite mercies put in every man today, regardless of race, color, religion or gender. Even though there is no longer communion with God as it was in the Garden, there is still a gentle voice of the loving Father asking the lost soul: "where art thou?" This is so that man would not be eternally lost without redemption. God said:

> *My spirit shall not always strive with man, for that he also is flesh. (Gen 6:3)*

The first display of God's act of redemption was to put man out of the Garden "lest he put forth his hand, and take also of the tree of life, and eat, and live for ever." (Gen 3:22)

The plan of God was to redeem Adam (mankind) and return him to the Garden to fulfill His mandate. But the devil was determined to truncate the plan by all means. Although he *successfully* edged man out of the Garden, but that is just for a season; the *spark* is the guiding light that will lead man back to the Garden of dominion, and God's eternal plan will be achieved.

In relation to time, we may think this is taking eternity to achieve but God is not bound by time. We may think the devil has been *winning* for a long time, but to God it's like few days, and besides, he is nowhere winning (Psa 90:4, 2Pe 3:8) God's plan will not fail, regardless. As always, Satan is still trying to out-do God, as if he really can.

Soul Dominance

When God warned Adam and Eve that they would die if they ate from the tree, they probably did not understand what it meant to die, because nobody ever died before then. They died anyway, a spiritual death. This death simply means that since they were created spirit beings (in the image and likeness of God), their original being (spirit man) died. They were from then on controlled by the soul. Their spiritual eyes became blind and the soul's eyes were opened. They became overtly conscious of themselves, their situation and their surroundings. This was contrary to their original nature that was conscious and full of God in the Garden. For the first time, they saw that they were **naked**. For the first time, they were **afraid** to hear the voice of God. Right there and then, Adam and Eve felt so much **shame** that they had to find something to cover their nakedness. All these experiences are attributes of the soul which they never manifested before. The reality of 'death' that God warned them about became apparent.

All Adam and Eve ever knew before in their pure spirit state and as pure spirit beings was God. This is what spirituality confers on man. But from the fall, they became soul-beings, no longer knowing God but "knowing good and evil." The "knowing" is derived from the discovery of self, not the revelation of God.

Discovery of self always prompts man to do something more to 'better' the self. This is because self is never satisfied with itself. Anyone possessed by self will always and forever be looking for something to "make up." Even when he is in the best state, he is still looking for something better.

We see this soulish act around us daily. It is a ministry which began with Lucifer. He was not satisfied with his state as the "son of the morning." He desired more than that. He wanted to be "like the Most High." He said in his heart:

> *I will ascend into heaven, I will exalt my throne above the stars of God: I will sit also upon the mount of the congregation, in the sides of the north: I will ascend above the heights of the clouds; I will be like the most High. (Isa 14:13-14)*

This is a heart issue. The heart, which was once dominated and controlled by the spirit, is now dominated by the soul. The soul always wants to gratify itself. It wants to fulfill the desires of the flesh. The only way to counter this is to "walk in the Spirit, and ye shall not fulfill the lust of the flesh." (Gal 5:16)

Since Adam and Eve just fell out of the spirit, they could no longer walk in the spirit. They could not resist the desire of the flesh. The spirit man died, and the soul-man lives. They must from then on, fulfill the compelling desire of the soul. They must "make up" for their tragic state of nakedness.

The glory of God cannot be stained or tainted by sin. Since then, the Shekinah glory of God, which covered Adam and Eve up until then, was removed. They became *uncovered*. Since they never experienced this before, "they sewed fig leaves together, and made themselves aprons." (Gen 3:22) This is a further descent.

However, in His mercies, "God made coats of skins, and clothed them." Adam and Eve from then had to depend on their wisdom and judgment, no longer on God.

This is what happens when a man falls out of the grace of God through sin. The Shekinah glory of God covering him is removed, and he is naked. Without repentance and forgiveness, he goes further down. This is fueled by the compelling power of the soul to lure man to try to make up or cover up. This is always the ministry of the soul. He brings man to this level and then drags him away from redemption. When a man operates at this level, it is an indication that the glory covering is removed.

This is what Cain also did when God called out to him: he tried to cover up. He said: *"Am I my brother's keeper?"* (Gen 4:9)

The Psalmist says:

> *He that covereth his sins shall not prosper: but whoso confesseth and forsaketh them shall have mercy. (Pro 28:13)*

Although there is an innate knowing in man that tells him he has missed the communion with God, and that he is out of place with God, but he is still devising various ways to cover his nakedness by his own effort. Just like Adam sowed fig leaves, man is putting together all kinds of things (religion) to cover up, rather than to go to God for redemption.

Before man fell, God already had a plan of redemption for him, for He knows all things, even that man would fall; He is

God. He already designed the way for man's return. Everything is according to His plan, purpose, and pleasure.

The truth is that man's wisdom is far too limited to comprehend this plan. Thus, he has substituted God's intention with his own intention to get back to God. Although it is a good and noble intention, but good is not God. Every good plan must align with God's divine purpose.

Religion and Faith

This good and noble way which man keeps devising to return to God is called religion. But God is not a God of religion but of Faith.

> *Without faith it is impossible to please him: for he that cometh to God must believe that he is, and that he is a rewarder of them that diligently seek him. (Heb 11:6)*

The way of redemption God made for man is through a Person, and not a system (Joh 3:16). God gave Jesus, not religion, or even Christianity. This Jesus had existed from the beginning. He is the spoken word. He "was in the beginning with God. All things were made by Him; and without Him was not anything made that was made. In Him was life; and the life was the light of men." (Joh 1:2-4). He was in the Garden of Eden as the tree of life. But Adam and Eve did not go to Him, rather, they went to the tree of knowledge of good and evil. If Adam and Eve had eaten from the tree of life before the fall, they would have lived forever in fulfillment. They would have been conformed to the image of life. But they chose the tree of death (the tree of the knowledge of good and evil) over the tree of life in the Garden. This is despite the fact that God warned them that they would die if they ate from it. They ate it anyway and they died as promised. They followed their "heart" rather than God. The heart is good; it can only choose good, not God, just as it was in the Garden.

Adam and Eve were sincere but guilty of their choice. In the same manner, man is sincere but guilty of the choices he makes without God.

> *For they being ignorant of God's righteousness, and going about to establish their own righteousness, have not submitted themselves unto the righteousness of God. (Rom 10:3)*

Good Intention
The good intention of man, made in utmost sincerity does not necessarily reflect God's intention. Many times, it looks good in isolation, but it is just a piece of the puzzle in the overall plan of God. One good plan that does not fit into the overall plan is as bad as it can be. The plan of God is supreme even when a piece of it is incomprehensible to man.

What precipitated the dispersal of man in the then world began as a good intention. Man simply wanted to build a city and tower to reach heaven so that they could make a name for themselves and so that they would not "be scattered abroad upon the face of the whole earth." (Gen 11:4) See how good that is? In a nutshell, Nimrod simply wanted to preserve the human race. He wanted the whole world to be in one place and grow together.

However, as good as this may sound, it is different from the original plan and intention of God for the world. God wanted man to "be fruitful, and multiply, and replenish the earth, and subdue it: and have dominion over the fish of the sea, and over the fowl of the air, and over every living thing that moveth upon the earth." (Gen 1:28) This is more or less a clash of interest. God wanted them to grow and spread around the world, but man wanted to be in one place. This led to confusion and division. At a time like this, God's will is supreme.

Meanwhile, Nimrod's intention was not as plain as it sounded. It was laced with a sinister plan and motive. It was a thought propelled by evil desire and spirit of control.

Man's will is evil because it comes from a diseased heart that cannot align with God. Therefore by default, man cannot choose right.

> *Every imagination of the thoughts of his heart was only evil continually. (Gen 6:5)*

It is interesting to know that Babel and denomination both point to the ability of man to do something great for God, man trying to help God build –man's good intention.

Many leaders today have sincere desire to preserve exclusive doctrines believed to be unique, germane and core to the faith of their group. Such leaders have their own churches, denominations and guiding laws to help members align with this vision. The truth is that as good as that may be, it's but a piece and must be reconciled with the overall plan of God to see if it fits, otherwise, it is as bad as it can be. No individual plan of man can align with God's overall plan except he allows God to play it out even when he does not understand it. That is when the struggle begins.

Thus, a good intention is not necessarily a God intention. The plan of many leaders may be good on its own, but again, good is not God. The question is that is it the same as the plan of Jesus Christ concerning His church? Jesus is the owner and builder of His church and knows exactly His plan: that "they may be one, even as we are one." (Joh 17:22) Any other good intention is not of God.

Without Jesus
As humans, however, to achieve the oneness and unity Jesus wants, especially in His Church without His Spirit is impossible. Jesus knows this and that is why He must build it by Himself. He will do that through us if we allow Him. Until the whole body, the church is fitly joined together and compacted and every part is effectually working in their measure so that all receive supplies from the head, there will be division within the body. (Eph 4:16)

The fruit of division is denominations. Denominations never crossed the mind of Christ in the building of His own Church. But today, we keep fomenting it. It has come to stay. This is because it is the ministry of man and the expression of individual calling, not necessarily the expression of the body of Christ. This is hard for Jesus to recognize, although we call it church. It is an innocent action in disobeying God just as it was in the Garden.

Building a central tower that reaches to God or breaking out of a denomination to begin a 'better' church for Christ seems like a good and reasonable thing to do, but God cannot accept what does not come from Him.

Many times, denomination is the show of man to convince himself and his followers that he is doing something for God. It is the sin of 'doing' something for God when God wants us to do nothing, but just be still, that is what is difficult for man.

Every founder of a denomination or movement always claims to receive leading or inspiration from God, often to restore the 'original' master plan, which they barely know. This buttresses the fact that religious fulfillment is an affront to God. God is a God of faith, not religion. Performance is the currency of religion and obedience is the currency of faith even when it seems ridiculous. The ridiculous brings the miraculous.

Abraham is called the father of faith, not the father of religion. But truly, we have made him the father of religion. Three of the world most popular religions claim origin from him: Judaism, Christianity, and Islam. God is called the God of Abraham, Isaac, and Jacob (persons), not the God of any religion. He is also called the God (Father) of our Lord Jesus Christ, not of Christianity. None of these religions leads to God. He is the God of persons, not systems. He is the God of the living, not of the dead. Abraham, Isaac, and Jacob pleased God "by faith," not by performance as we see today (Heb 11).

It is not God that gave us Christianity (He gave us a Person). This Person is building His church as "...One body, and One Spirit... One hope ... One Lord, One faith, One baptism, One God..." (Eph 4:4-6) Hence, there is only one true church, the church that Jesus builds. It is not a denomination. It is not headed, founded or owned by man, has no corporate branches or headquarter, and it cannot be founded or joined. Jesus is the Head and the Builder, yet He invites us to be part of the process, consistent with His character.

Everything God is doing is "according to His good pleasure which He hath purposed in himself." (Eph 1:9). This is the mystery of His will, "that in all things he might have the preeminence." (Col 1:18) God will be all in all, in all things, not all in some, in some things. Yet, He is involving man in the process.

Man's Ability
How can man know what God is doing when he has tremendous ability of his own to do something marvelous for God and ask God to come and see and accept it? How can he recognize his role and his involvement in what God is doing? This has been the bane of man in cooperating with God.

Satan is always magnifying man's ability and his tremendous potential for him to see. He always pushes man to use his innate power to achieve great heights. This is soulish. Jesus clearly told His disciples: "without me, you can do nothing." (Joh 15:5) But there is always a great inner urge to do something. Yet, when 'something' is done, it appears perfect and acceptable to man.

When Samuel was to anoint a new king for Israel, he went into the house of Jesse. When he saw Eliab, one of the sons of Jesse, the great prophet Samuel said:

> *Surely the Lord's anointed is before him. But the Lord said unto Samuel, Look not on his countenance, or on the height of his stature; because I have refused him: for the Lord seeth not as man seeth; for man looketh on the outward appearance, but the Lord looketh on the heart. (1Sa 16:6-7)*

As we can see, the wisdom of man is foolishness with God. The things that are hailed by man are abominations to the Lord (1Co 1:27-28, Luk 16:15). We need to reconcile this with the great cathedrals, beautiful altars, and wonderful services, programs and activities we give to the Lord. God does not see the way man sees. The offering of Cain may be beautiful to the eyes and functional, but there is a content God is looking for. That is why many miss Jesus, because "there is no beauty that we should desire Him," but Isaiah prophetically says that God shall see the travail of His soul and He shall be satisfied (Isa 53:2, 11). Man is looking for beauty, God is looking for travail. The cross is still the emblem of salvation, not the crown. If you look for the crown, it must be laced with thorns.

Like the popular adage: "the dog has no new tricks," so also Satan. He still uses the same primordial strategy he used in the Garden to destroy Adam and Eve:

> *Hath God said, Ye shall not eat of every tree of the garden? ... And the serpent said unto the woman, Ye shall not surely die: For God doth know that in the day ye eat thereof, then your eyes shall be opened, and ye shall be as gods, knowing good and evil. (Gen 3:1,4-5)*

Satan's strategy is to magnify the potential and the ability of man and then charge him to do something with it. That's why he is the lord of this (new) age. This goes as far as our relationship with God, especially when we birth new believers into the kingdom. We charge them to work for God rather than to walk with God. This explains the magnificent structures, beautiful altars, wonderful overseas missions which many support with a feel of satisfaction that they are working for God. These are good but do not replace the relationship with Jesus. It leads to performance –use of talent rather than gifts of the Spirit. Talent is our ability but gift is God's ability in us through His Spirit and for His glory.

Moses wanted to fulfill God's call in his life through his talent, but he failed. He had to wait for another forty years to fulfill the call.

This ideology, which has its root in the soul is eating deep into the fabric of the life of believers and the church has sadly replaced the understanding of working for God.

Some people asked Jesus:

> *What shall we do, that we might work the works of God? Jesus answered and said unto them, This*

> *is the work of God, that ye believe on him whom he hath sent. (Joh 6:28-29)*

Jesus' answer doesn't look like work to us. Whether that is true or not is not the issue, the most important thing is to stop where God stops, "to obey is better than to sacrifice." (1Sa 15:22)

When God told Adam and Eve not to eat from the tree of the knowledge of good and evil, they never knew it would be as subtle as just an introduction to try their ability. Many think that as long as you don't take the evil from the good and evil, you stay just with the good, then, you are not participating in the evil. This is a smart thinking, which is generally called 'positive thinking.' But the truth is that we do not relate to God by thoughts but by revelation. No matter how positive our thoughts are, they have roots in the soul because thought is an attribute of the soul, and Satan is the lord of the soul realm.

Beyond the 'good' in the tree is a magnitude of evil impossible to see or imagine by mortals. Eve knew what they should not do, but could not resist the urge that magnified the tremendous power and opportunities she would enjoy in doing it. Satan's strategy is still the same up till now: he urges and leads people into performance. To demonstrate the ability to do great things for God: organize crusades, church planting, church growth, build institutions and so on. These activities are more of display of status for many denominations today. It may be good with wonderful result but has to be reconciled if it is by leading or burden.

While the spirit-man becomes dormant, the soul-man becomes dominant. The soul leads in a beautiful highway of destruction (Pro 16:25). This is because Satan seemingly moves ahead of God in everything: he always presents his own fireworks before God's still small voice. He comes to the Garden before God comes in the cool of the day. The purpose is to present a working alternative that is equally viable, comparable, fruitful, and almost undetectable compared with the original.

The good intention of man, no matter how noble, is not the same as the sovereign plan of God. Man has tremendous ability to do so well what should not be done at all. Even though it looks perfect, it doesn't make it of God. Our opinion in the things of God does not matter as His instruction, just like what the sheep is thinking of the lion does not matter to the lion. We must ensure that we build according to pattern. If it does not come from God, it cannot return to God.

We must do away with all man-made and man-led movements, organizations, and programs, which tend to help God by performance. We must rather enter into His rest, and by faith allow Him to do what He alone can do. This is quite challenging in the face of great ideas and ability in man begging to offer something beautiful, presentable, acceptable and workable for God. It is a good intention but not necessarily God's. It is not in the size of what we offer but the obedience. This knowledge is the first step in unlocking the secret of experiencing the fullness and the totality of God.

3

PARTNERSHIP

"We are labourers together with God: ye are God's husbandry, ye are God's building."
- **1 Corinthians 3:9**

Grace by Faith

THERE ARE MANY religions offering salvation to man. Many of these come with great cost, and at the end, a great loss. But the salvation that comes from God to man is a free gift: it is not dependent on man's effort or work.

> *For by grace are ye saved through faith; and that not of yourselves: it is the gift of God: Not of works, lest any man should boast. (Eph 2:8-9)*

Although, it is free to man, however, it is at great cost to God. The only *cost* as it were, to man is for him to simply take the gift by faith. That is man's own part, 'work' or involvement in the process of salvation from God. This is what Paul means when he says, "...work out your own salvation with fear and trembling." (Phi 2:12b) "Fear and trembling" means to be diligent and guard the precious free gift so that it does not slip away (Mat 25, Heb 2:1). This can only be achieved through a trusting faith in the power of the Holy Spirit in us as we yield to Him.

So we see the *manifold* grace of God towards man. Although, He is all in all and did everything for man in His grace and omnipotence, yet He still involves man in the process. Grace is to God as faith is to man. God gives grace but man must respond in faith for the grace to be effective. Paul in 1Cor. 3:9 says, "we are laborers *together with* God: ye are God's husbandry, ye are God's building." In 2Co 6:1, he says, "we then, as workers *together with* him..." The involvement of man in what God is doing is the process where man can **experience God** and come into **His reality**. God initiated and demonstrated this in Eden with Adam and Eve (Gen 3:8). Even though in effect, it is man's part, it is God's design nonetheless.

According to Pattern

The first step in the overall plan of God's redemption of man is for man to come to Him -in His terms, not ours. We cannot approach Him with our own design, pattern or idea. It will bring further separation and alienation from God. We may offer great praise or soaking worship songs in an emotion-laden atmosphere; we may be involved in charity in many nations; labor to bring souls into the kingdom in droves, or even champion a course for Christ, but God will only accept what comes from Himself: His design and pattern (1Co 13:1-3, Rev 2:2-7). Only what comes from Him can stand and return to Him.

We must understand this unchangeable nature and character of God. Even though we find it innovative to give Him styles we consider fanciful, befitting and honorable, we cannot change His order. We may deploy all sorts of styles to win souls but God has His own way to save the souls. They belong to Him, not us.

Uzzah and Ahio were *innocently* slain for trying to give God a more decent and befitting new style. They drove the Ark of the Covenant in a new cart rather than carry it on the shoulders (2Sa 6:2-7). He is an ancient God and we cannot modernize Him, His presence, worship, fellowship or meetings with our inventions, tools or equipment. He wants us more than what we can give to Him. What do we have to give to Him? We cannot ask Him to accept what we have done for Him or what we feel is right for Him. His will is His will and it is supreme.

Cain offered his best to God. But God is not asking for our best but our obedience. There is something that He is looking for in our offerings and sacrifices. For instance, God would not approve or convert Paul's labor and passion for the Jews as an acceptable ministry (Rom 9:3), even when he labored intensely with astounding success for them. All would be in vain because he was not sent to them per se, but to the Gentiles. Peter experienced the same challenge: he labored with the Gentiles, whereas he was sent to the Jews. Until they individually came in alignment with God's order, regardless of their passion and burden, it remained their ministry, not God's.

Zeal and passion do not appease God, in the same way that we cannot present our plans before God for His approval or rubber-stamping. Abraham attempted it with Ishmael: he begged God to forget Isaac (God's plan), and bless Ishmael instead (his own work and effort, Gen 17:18). This is what happens when we ask God to make our will His. We must rather pray that His will be ours.

When we are willing to come to God on His terms, it is then we are beginning to chart the course of a normal walk with God. That can only be done in faith and obedience, not in works and effort. Only then can we become part and parcel of His eternal plan. We become an integral part of His purpose. We become joint-heirs of His heritage. We come into the reality and experience of Him. We can say we are laborers together *with* God and not laborers *for* God. This has always been the desire of God.

God is bidding us come to Him that we may together be partakers of the inheritance of the saints in light and that He may show us His ways and His acts. That is when the prayer: "Thy will be done on earth as it is in heaven" becomes true.

Man, however, always chooses the abnormal path right from Eden. When God came down to deliver Israel from Egypt, He promised to be their God but Israel didn't want that. Their excuse was that His presence was too fearful and terrifying. Rather, they nominated Moses as the [middle] man between them and God. That is always the character of man; he chooses what he wants over what God ordains. However, God is always a patient God, He gave Israel His permissive, not perfect will. He granted Israel's request and allowed Moses to be the go-between.

Even at that, God warned Moses to "make sure you build the tabernacle according to the pattern which was shewed thee on the mount." (Exo 25:40) Moses was diligent with this charge, but Israel rebelled again and again. They chose their own pattern through fear and unbelief. Consequently, they could not enter into God's rest.

In these last days, man is walking in the same spirit: he chooses his own pattern, worship, service, and religion. He is building his own church and negotiating his own terms of coming to God. He is concerned with quantity, whereas God is concerned with quality. He ignores God's set pattern and the normal cycle of the Christian life. He thrives on mere tradition, own doctrines, plans and strategies of the religious institutions. But it is not about what man says God says; this is theology: it is what God says. There is the normal cycle designed by God and there is another designed by man that looks like the normal but it is not. Only the spirit of Christ in a believer can tell the difference. God's way requires a working out by faith.

The Process of Time
It is possible for God to design a way of salvation for man without the rigors of allowing Jesus to come to the earth to work it out. When God told the Serpent that, "I will put enmity between thee and the woman, and between thy seed and her seed; it shall bruise thy head, and thou shalt bruise his heel," (Gen 3:15) God could have made this to happen the

next minute, hour, day or year. Why did it take Him thousands of years to work it out?

We have to understand that everything of God requires a process of time, and God is a patient God. If He waited for four thousand to fulfill the promise He gave to Eve in Eden, He sure can wait a long time to fulfill His purpose. This is because He is building an enduring work. Quality takes time.

When Satan approached Jesus and offered Him the world just for a bow, why didn't Jesus save Himself the trouble and agony of going through Golgotha and dying on the rugged cross to save humanity? Couldn't He have just accepted Satan's offer and work it for the good purpose?

Since Jesus left to prepare a place for us in His Father's house, so that where He is, we also will be, why has it taken Him this long to return and take His bride away with Him? Why did Jesus not just take anyone that believes to heaven immediately he or she receives Him as Lord and Savior?

The answer to these questions is that there is always a process of time in everything. God does not cut corners. The life of a true believer requires a process, not necessarily a program. There is a cycle and you cannot jump it. Even Jesus said:

> *The cup, which my Father hath given me, shall I not drink it? (Joh 18:11)*

Believers must beware of fast lane ministries or teachers that promise quick return on investment. Giving your life to Jesus may be a high-yield investment but it is nonetheless a high-risk investment. It is the first in the series of many processes.

It does no good if you come to Christ and not walk with Him, or if you walk with Him but do not mature in Him. There is a normal cycle you must not only aspire to know but follow. That is your own part in the scheme of God. It is God's ordained pattern, not yours, or any leader's denomination or movement. What did not originate from God cannot culminate with Him.

Unity

Jesus Christ is building a church that consists of many members in one body. Just like our physical body consists of many members and organs but all functioning together in harmony to make a total body.

> *For as we have many members in one body, and all members have not the same office: So we, being many, are one body in Christ, and every one members one of another. (Rom 12:4-5)*

This is a difficult task for man to achieve by himself. This is because each member has his or her own will, mind, thoughts, desire, and so on. They are all of different background, personality, conviction, persuasions and so on, yet they must agree and work in harmony as one. How can that be possible? With man, it is impossible but with God all things are possible.

This is the challenge the Church is facing today and this is why there are denominations and there will ever be denominations springing up every day. Statistics reveal that there are several thousand denominations, and new ones are springing up almost at an hour interval worldwide.

If every man who claims to be called by God into ministry will allow Jesus to do it His own way, there will be unity and oneness in the body, and the church of Jesus will be one. But everyone is building according to his conviction, beliefs, and passion, sincerely destroying the fabric in which the church was sewed, which is oneness.

It was difficult then for Israel to just allow God whom they did not see to be their King. They wanted to be 'like other nations' with human kings to rule them. It is difficult for the church today too, to allow Jesus through the Holy Spirit whom she does not see physically to lead her.

When Moses, the God's chosen one for Israel went up the mountain to meet with God on behalf of the people, Israel chose another leader for themselves before he returned.

> *The people gathered themselves together unto Aaron, and said unto him, Up, make us gods, which shall go before us; for as for this Moses, the man that brought us up out of the land of Egypt, we wot not what is become of him. (Exo 32:1)*

Waiting on Him

The truth is that God is never early, but He is never late. Many times, it is tiring to wait on God. Elijah is a [living] witness. He expected God for several days, but God did not show up until he gave up (1Ki 19:11-12).

When we wait on God in our quiet time, it is every easy to drift off or rise without hearing anything. He is not in our hurry. Sometimes He delays because He is killing our flesh.

The flesh is for pleasure and wants everything to be quick and easy. This is why in our meetings, we always have a program drawn out to follow so we would not have to wait for the Holy Spirit, who may not be too tied up to our timing, or understand our schedule. Yet, it is in waiting on Him that our strength lies.

Jesus told His disciples when He was ascending up to glory:

> *And, behold, I send the promise of my Father upon you: but tarry ye in the city of Jerusalem, until ye be endued with power from on high. (Luk 24:49)*

For the disciples to function and be one, they must wait for the Holy Spirit for as long as it would take Him to come. What if the Holy Spirit would not come? They must not attempt to do anything by themselves without Him. They must tarry until… How faithful are believers or the church to this? We make things happen so that we will not disappoint the expectant congregation, we don't want to be called powerless or give room for our calling to be doubted, or lose the members.

The reason why the church must tarry for the Holy Spirit is because it is Him that will build the church, not us. The church is supposed to be one: one body, one Spirit, one hope, one Lord, one faith, one baptism and one God (Eph 4:4-6). But today, it is obvious who is building the church, and as long as that continues, and it is likely it does, there will be no unity and oneness. There are many ministries with multiple services on a Sunday. Everything has to be quick so that they can accommodate the crowd. It has to be to time, the people's time, not the Holy Spirit's time. It seems that the days of waiting on Him are over, now He must wait on us!

Aaron made the golden calf for the people because that was what they demanded. Although, he knew what God demanded, but the quest to please the people was his major drive. He also wanted to be relevant to the people and not be stoned (Exo 32). It is the same thing today; the major drive of many ministries or leaders is the people. Programs are for the people, the fellowships are for the people, special super services are for the people, the messages are for the people, the timing, music, planning and so on are all for the people.

Isn't this consistent with the words of Apostle Paul:

> *For the time will come when they will not endure sound doctrine; but after their own lusts shall they heap to themselves teachers, having itching ears; And they shall turn away their ears from the truth, and shall be turned unto fables. (2Ti 4:3-4)*

We must understand that the Church is not a democracy: church of the people, for the people, by the people; it is a theocracy; it is the church of the living God and Jesus is the builder. It is not instituted by votes, loyalty or performance, but by the Holy Spirit. It may be religiously good but not spiritually sound when we ask people to join a department within the church in order to build the church or work for God. That is building a denomination and that is neither God's priority nor concern. It is helping a man build his vision and empire in the name of a church; such, God would rather tear down. It is the same as babel.

The time is here! Ministers are to minister God's mind and instruction to the people, not to minister to the people the desires of their hearts. This is a soulish operation.

Dead Men Wanted
For the Holy Spirit to build the church, we must get out of the scene, we must decrease (Joh 3:30), if we don't, God cannot work in us and through us. If God did not cause Adam to have a 'deep-sleep,' He could not bring out Eve from his side (Ge 2:21). It was when Christ also *slept* that the church was born. We must go into this deep sleep so God can operate in us to bring His best out of us.

God is looking for dead men, only in them can He deposit His Spirit. Only these men can be broken enough to work in love, for he that is dead no longer cares for the things of this world, he abides at wherever he is led to. As long as man wants to be in control, there cannot be one church, but several denominations of people who are not in unity or one accord with each other but their local selves. That is a powerless church, a church built by man, such, the gate of hell can still prevail against. Only the Church of Jesus does the gate of hell has no power over.

The partnership God requires from us is to know His plan so that we can do our part. He has made the feast ready, He bids us come to dine with Him. Yet, in dining with Him, He required of us to comply with His rules.

God's Grace

In the parable of the king that made a banquet for his friends, those whom he invited did not come. They had different excuses and reasons:

> ...The first said unto him, I have bought a piece of ground, and I must needs go and see it: I pray thee have me excused. And another said, I have bought five yoke of oxen, and I go to prove them: I pray thee have me excused. And another said, I have married a wife, and therefore I cannot come. (Luk 14:18-20)

This prophetically refers to Israel, who rejected God's invitation. The king, therefore, told His servants: "Go out quickly into the streets and lanes of the city, and bring in hither the poor, and the maimed, and the halt, and the blind." This prophetically refers to the gentiles -the church. Even though God chose Israel, but because Israel rejected the invitation, God invited the Gentiles (the church) to become partakers of the life and grace of God, which Israel lost.

As said earlier, grace requires faith to be effective. If those who were not part of the original plan of the king to attend the feast but were invited by the king's generosity and benevolence did not accept the invitation, they could never be part of the king's banquet. Paul said:

> But now in Christ Jesus ye who sometimes were far off are made nigh by the blood of Christ. (Eph 2:13)

This refers to the Gentiles. We must accept the King's invitation with gratitude and faith, knowing that we are not qualified to dine with Him in the first place. Part of the way to show gratitude is to keep the feast, but more importantly, to be dressed in the proper garment, the garment that the King has chosen for His own feast.

The grace of God has brought the Gentiles into the King's domain (kingdom). But the grace must not be abused. If we come in through illegal way or abnormal route (which is very possible – John 10), we have abused the grace, we have rejected the way of God and following our own effort, jumping the fence or breaking in through the window. Those who do such are thieves and robbers. We must respond in faith, which is absolute trust in the way the king has made for everybody to come into His palace. We must remember that before He called us, we were without Christ, "aliens to the commonwealth of Israel, and strangers from the covenants of promise, having no hope, and without God in the world: But now in Christ Jesus ye who sometimes were far off are made nigh by the blood of Christ." (Eph 2:12-13) This is who we were and that is why the grace of God is abundant on us because where sin abounds, grace abounds much more. (Rom 5:20)

God reconciled us to Himself through the death of Jesus and called us in. Having then obtained such a wonderful grace from God, it requires us to come through the legal way and also to be dressed in the proper garment the king has chosen. We must do away with our traditional garment and cultural dresses so that we can be acceptable to the King.

However, there are touts all around who claim to have the ability to take people into the Kings' banquet on a joy ride, fanfare, ecstasy and mass entry. Truly, they can. What they cannot do is to give such people the wedding garment. That is the exclusive function of the Prince - Jesus. Be careful so you do not fall victim of many touts in the kingdom.

Wedding Garment

Jesus closed the parable by saying that despite the King's benevolence, there was still someone in the banquet who abused it:

> *And when the king came in to see the guests, he saw there a man which had not on a wedding garment: And he saith unto him, Friend, how camest thou in hither not having a wedding-garment? And he was speechless. Then said the king to the servants, Bind him hand and foot, and take him away, and cast him into outer darkness; there shall be weeping and gnashing of teeth. (Mat 22:11-13)*

This man represents believers who, though entered the kingdom, but did not enter through the normal process. Being a welcome guest in this feast means that you must not only come in through the gate, but you must also have a wedding garment. The gate is Christ and the garment is the righteousness of Christ.

This, not just a parable, it is a prophetic message for the last day's church. We have been invited into the kingdom, but we must come through the proper way. We must be born into the kingdom. "Except a man be born again, he cannot enter the kingdom of God." (Joh 3:3)

Many truly enter through the gate. This means that they have at one time or the other responded to the spark of God calling out to them. The man without the wedding garment at the feast represent those who at one time or the other have responded to the message of salvation and have come forward in altar call or personally, and took the step of faith in coming to the kingdom through the born again experience. This is commendable and the heaven rejoices. But that is just the first step. You may still be sent away before the feast is over. The kingdom requires being clothed with a garment, absolute righteousness.

> *For the kingdom of God is not meat and drink; but righteousness, and peace, and joy in the Holy Ghost. (Rom 14:17)*

Many truly profess Christ today, but there is no righteousness of Christ in them. All they have is the testimony that they at one time or the other responded to the invitation to the banquet of the king and they kept the feast. That is a good testimony. But remember that this man that was bundled out of the feast also kept the feast. It is not that he did not have a garment; he had his own garment, which is even worse than not having any at all. He came with his own righteousness, which as we see could not save him even though he made it to the kingdom. It is one thing to make it to the kingdom (which is always a free invitation), but to continue to be in the kingdom has a cost, and it is righteousness. Alas! Our own righteousness is filthy rags before God.

Paul said:

> *And be found in him, not having mine own righteousness, which is of the law, but that which is through the faith of Christ, the righteousness which is of God by faith. (Php 3:9)*

This righteousness can only be gotten by the Spirit of Christ through the born again experience.

Jesus did not stop at asking Nicodemus to be born again, He went further to say that "except a man be born of water and the spirit…"

The "water and the Spirit" confer the righteousness on the believer to be able to experience all, not just a part of God. This is the difference between those who claim to be born again and those who are actually born again. The latter are those who are baptized in the spirit. If you are yet to be baptized in the spirit, even though you have responded to the call and experienced the joy of salvation, you do not yet possess the wedding garment, the righteousness of Jesus. The good news is that you can get it before it is too late.

Spirit baptism confers on you the righteousness and semblance of Jesus in the kingdom. When God looks at you in the kingdom, He does not see you but Jesus. He sees the righteousness (garment) of His Son, not your works. Your best works are filthy rags to Him. It is what Christ did on the cross of Calvary for your sake alone. That is your only take Paul long to know. The things of the spirit are spirits and they are spiritually discerned. It will be obvious for anyone with the Holy Spirit to know that something is amiss in such gathering or fellowship.

These disciples at Ephesus were sincere, but they could have died in their sincere ignorance, and they wouldn't have been part of what God is doing, and so cannot reign with Him. They were not baptized into life but rituals. They must have been singing songs and experiencing 'something' and thought they were in. If they had followed John and his teachings through, they would have known that John himself said someone was coming after him who would baptize them with spirit and with life. That was the exact challenge Paul gave them:

> *Then said Paul, John verily baptized with the baptism of repentance, saying unto the people, that they should believe on him which should come after him, that is, on Christ Jesus. (Act 19:4)*

The difference between these disciples and today's disciples is that:

> *When they heard this, they were baptized in the name of the Lord Jesus. And when Paul had laid his hands upon them, the Holy Ghost came on them; and they spake with tongues, and prophesied. And all the men were about twelve. (Act 19:5-7)*

If you fall into the same category as these disciples, what you are reading now is the word of the Lord to you. The Lord is telling you that you need extra oil to sustain you till the last days, and for the end time apostasy, which is already here now. You may have goose bumps during many praise and worship sessions or gatherings, but that does not mean the Holy Spirit is present. Often, we confuse mere emotions with reality. The Holy Spirit is a real Being, neither a thing nor a feeling. When you have Him, He will take the things of the Father and make it yours. Your experience will be real and sustainable, not like a dream.

The disciples in Ephesus were humble enough to listen to Paul, and they "were baptized in the name of the Lord Jesus," not in any other strange name, not in the titles of the Trinity, but in the NAME of Jesus Christ.

David Pawson, in his book, explains and put to rest the age-long controversy about baptizing either in the name of the Father, Son, and the Holy Spirit or in the name of Jesus. According to him:

> *One of the main reasons given for this attribution is that the Trinitarian wording of Matthew 28:19-20 is more reminiscent of ecclesiastical formulae and is at variance with the use of the name of Jesus by itself throughout the book of Acts (e.g. Acts 8:16; 19:5). Certainly, there is no direct evidence of the use of the Trinitarian formula in baptism until the second century AD.*
>
> *If the form of immersion in water was the same for the apostles as it had been for John the Baptist, the formula used was certainly different. Indeed,*

> *the use of name in baptism was clearly an apostolic innovation. The Matthean formula is usually assumed to contain three names: 'Father', 'Son' and 'Holy Spirit'. But this simple reading of the phrase is, in fact, too simplistic – for the following reasons:*
>
> 1. *Technically, 'Father' and 'Son' are not 'names', but relationships.*
> 2. *The 'name' of the Father is 'Yahweh', from which comes 'Jehovah'.*
> 3. *The 'name' of the Son is 'Jesus'.*
> 4. *The word 'name' is in the singular (one), not in the plural (three)*
>
> *However, the main problem with the 'three names' position comes from the fact that though Trinitarian benedictions and used by the apostles (e.g. IICor 13:14), there is no record of any Trinitarian baptisms in the New Testament. These, like all healings and deliverances, were done on the single, powerful name of 'Jesus' only. How do we explain this apparent discrepancy?* [i]

While this doctrine (or any other) must not determine our fellowship or divide our oneness in Christ, it is good to know that water baptism is total immersion in water, and spirit baptism is total immersion in the power of the Holy Ghost. After the 'disciples' were baptized in water, Paul later laid hands on them and they received the Holy Spirit, with physical evidence of speaking in tongues.

As said earlier, the Holy Spirit is not something, He is Someone, He is the Spirit of God Himself. You cannot think you have Him, you will know if you have Him. He fills you up. He intoxicates you with love for Jesus, not zeal, excited utterances, enticing words of man's wisdom, display of emotions and so on. Paul challenged the church at Corinth:

> *Examine yourselves, whether ye be in the faith; prove your own selves. Know ye not your own selves, how that Jesus Christ is in you, except ye be reprobates? (2Co 13:5)*

Please, if you have repented of your wickedness (not being in the camp of God) and have confessed Christ as not only Savior but also Lord, get baptized in water; it will help you in your faith walk. More importantly, get baptized in the Spirit. It is better to look for the oil now while it is still day, the night cometh when no one will be able to work (Joh 9:4). When the door will be shut and He is no longer available.

Without the Holy Spirit, you cannot worship God in spirit and in truth. Your service is mere religion and you have no hope of Rapture. It is not too late to get the Holy Spirit, He is your passport to partnering with Christ to make His kingdom come.

4

THE CYCLE

*"To everything there is a season,
and a time to every purpose under the heaven."*
- **Ecclesiastes 3:1**

The Heart of the Father

THE WORDS OF Ecclesiastes (3:1) buttresses the fact that it is not only life that has a cycle, but also "anything" and "every purpose." This cycle is separated by times and seasons. This is also true of the spiritual experience in God. He wants us to pass through the *times and seasons* (process) of the born again experience that culminates in salvation.

The word "salvation" (Greek, *sozo*) is an all-encompassing word. It means *"to heal, cure, to make well; to rescue from danger, to save; to cause something to change to an earlier, correct or appropriate state; to renew."* It means deliverance, victory in all areas of life and endeavor, and soul, spirit, and body. John said:

> *Beloved, I wish above all things that thou mayest prosper and be in health, even as thy soul prospereth (3Jo 1:2)*

This experience will make us a proven child of God that has truly overcome the enemy. It will make us a child of God that He is proud of and can vouch for. It will make us a true overcomer that can defeat the adversary. We become children that have matured to the fullness of the stature of Christ and the true image and likeness of our Father -God; to rule and reign. It is thus necessary for us to pass through all the junctions of experience in order to attain this.

In the beginning in the Garden of Eden, man possessed this ability to enable him fulfill the eternal plan of God so that as God rules and reigns in heaven, man, as a child of God would rule and reign on earth, too. And also to have fellowship and communion with God, and to worship Him (Gen 2:16-17). God's primary call for man is to be in Him, walk with Him and mature in Him. This is because God desires relationship with man in order to fulfill His purpose in Him. But man lost it to the adversary. He can no longer have dominion or have fellowship with God again.

But as believers today, we must understand the heart of God: He wants to return us to the original plan, and we must cooperate with Him. The adversary will fight tooth and nail to prevent this. This is the reason why we cannot afford to jump any experience in the faith walk. Every junction gives different graces, weapons and fire-power to overcome and return to the rightful place of authority.

The Beginning of War

Outside the Garden, Adam and Eve must make another choice still: to go out of the Garden, perhaps to the city of Nod in the east of the Garden (where Cain earlier went to marry his wife, Gen 4:16), or remain on their own in a new territory they have just been sent to by God and perhaps contend further with the serpent.

God had earlier made a pronouncement that a seed would come from the woman to bruise the serpent's head. Knowing this, the serpent was poised to make sure that the promised seed would not survive. The spiritual lesson in this is that Satan will with all his power to prevent a believer from entering into God's promise or attaining destiny. In the book of Revelation:

> *The dragon stood before the woman which was ready to be delivered, for to devour her child as soon as it was born. And she brought forth a man child, who was to rule all nations with a rod of iron: and her child was caught up unto God, and to his throne. And the woman fled into the wilderness, where she hath a place prepared of God, that they should feed her there a thousand two hundred and threescore days. (Rev 12:4-6)*

Although, this is a future event, but it is the continuation of the war with the woman to prevent the promised Seed from returning to the Garden, and it is far from ending. Right from that time and up till Calvary, to the time of the great tribulation, down through the battle of Armageddon, Satan has been turning every stone to destroy the Seed. He keeps devising ways to achieve his plans but he keeps failing. He thought since he scuttled the original plan for man to rule the earth (which he thought belonged to him by default), it was the end. He did not bargain for the promise of *another* seed. Down through the ages and up till Calvary, his onerous task was to prevent the seed from coming. He failed at each attempt.

His Restiveness
Again, Satan must have thought that he succeeded when Israel did not accept Jesus as the Messiah, but rather killed Him. The meaning of Calvary was totally hidden from him. To him, it was the place to destroy the Seed of the woman permanently. He did not realize that it is in the original plan of God to save the whole world, not just Israel. He will bring other fold to Himself, the Gentiles (Joh 1:16). Without Calvary, there will be no salvation for the Gentiles. This is the main reason why Israel was "blinded in part" (by God) and rejected the Messiah (Rom 11:25).

How amazing to know that even Satan is working according to God's plans and purposes. No wonder God referred to some wicked kings like Nebuchadnezzar as His servants. While he thinks that he is pursuing his own brilliant task, he is actually *helping* God achieve His overall plan: that God will be all in all (Phi 3:21b). When he instigated Israel against her Messiah who was supposed to lead her to the kingdom, hardly did he realize that he was dancing to the rhythm of God's eternal beat. The word of Apostle Paul is true:

> *And we know that all things work together for good to them that love God, to them who are the called according to his purpose. (Rom 8:28)*

The whole world sinned through Adam. God's plan is to redeem the whole world, not just a select few, race or tribe, not just Israel.

> *Wherefore, as by one man sin entered into the world, and death by sin; and so death passed upon all men, for that all have sinned... But not as the offence, so also is the free gift. For if through the offence of one many be dead, much more the grace of God, and the gift by grace, which is by one man, Jesus Christ, hath abounded unto many. And not as it was by one that sinned, so is the gift: for the judgment was by one to condemnation, but the free gift is of many offences unto justification. For if by one man's offence death reigned by one; much more they which receive abundance of grace and of the gift of righteousness shall reign in life by one, Jesus Christ.) Therefore as by the offence of one judgment came upon all men to condemnation; even so by the righteousness of one the free gift came upon all men unto justification of life. For as by one man's disobedience many were made sinners, so by the obedience of one shall many be made righteous. (Rom 5:12-19)*

Paul reiterated this truth to the Corinthian Church:

> *For since by man came death, by man came also the resurrection of the dead. For as in Adam all die, even so in Christ shall all be made alive. (1Co 15:21-22)*

But God began this redemptive work with Israel, and then to the whole world. This truth was blinded to Satan: his focus was on destroying Israel, but God has other plans that he is not aware of.

After several attempts of failing to destroy Israel in order to prevent the promised Seed from being born, now that He was born in a manger, contrary to his belief (he was probably looking into a palace), Satan shifted to trying to discredit the legitimacy of the birth of the seed. He knew that this would cause Israel to reject Him. He moved Joseph to reject Mary's pregnancy. He failed. After Jesus was born, he moved the wise men to uncover His identity to Herod, so that He might be killed. Although, the "wise men" did it with a good intention, but Satan cashed in on it. (Good intention is not God intention). He failed in this, too. He moved Israel through her leaders, to not only reject Jesus as the Messiah, but to kill Him by crucifixion, a public humiliation. It was a perfect strike for him, but little did he know that he was opening a channel of God's redemptive work for the gentiles.

Through Jesus's vicarious death on the cross, He became a curse and atoned for the sins of the whole world, for without the shedding of blood, there is no remission of sin. (Heb 9:22)

Having failed in all his attempts to destroy Jesus, Satan is still not giving up; he has one more joker in his sleeves. He knows that the Seed will still return to Israel at the end of The Great Tribulation in order to complete His mission (Jesus' second coming), so he is still not giving up yet. This is the time when he would gather the whole world to war with Him. John describes his final attempts:

> *And when the dragon saw that he was cast unto the earth, he persecuted the woman which brought forth the man child. And to the woman were given two wings of a great eagle, that she might fly into the wilderness, into her place, where she is nourished for a time, and times, and half a time, from the face of the serpent. And the serpent cast out of his mouth water as a flood after the woman, that he might cause her to be carried away of the flood. And the earth helped the woman, and the earth opened her mouth, and swallowed up the flood which the dragon cast out of his mouth. And the dragon was wroth with the woman, and went to make war with the remnant of her seed, which keep the commandments of God, and have the testimony of Jesus Christ. (Rev 12:13-17)*

John further described that he would deceive the whole world, with all the kings and rulers, and lead them to war with Jesus in a final battle (Armageddon) after The Great Tribulation:

> *And the sixth angel poured out his vial upon the great river Euphrates; and the water thereof was dried up, that the way of the kings of the east might be prepared. And I saw three unclean spirits like frogs come out of the mouth of the dragon, and out of the mouth of the beast, and out of the mouth of the false prophet. For they are the spirits of devils, working miracles, which go forth unto the kings of the earth and of the whole world, to gather them to the battle of that great day of God Almighty. Behold, I come as a thief. Blessed is he that watcheth, and keepeth his garments, lest he walk naked, and they see his shame.*
>
> *And he gathered them together into a place called in the Hebrew tongue Armageddon.*
> *(Rev 16:13-16)*

So we see that Satan is not resting, but God has given us rest. Although power has been given to him to wage war against the saints, the seed and the holy city, but the battle is the Lord's, not ours, yet we are His war-clubs and weapons of war (Jer 51:20). God's right hand has given Him victory. Therefore, we are fighting from victory, not for victory.

Weapons of Warfare
Paul wrote to the church at Corinth about the on-going war of Satan even with the saints at this hour:

> *For though we walk in the flesh, we do not war after the flesh: (For the weapons of our warfare*

> *are not carnal, but mighty through God to the pulling down of strong holds;) Casting down imaginations, and every high thing that exalteth itself against the knowledge of God, and bringing into captivity every thought to the obedience of Christ. (2Co 10:3-5)*

Our overcoming this warfare is a two-way action: by the Lord, and by us. Remember, God is always involving man in everything that He is doing.

> *And they overcame him by the blood of the Lamb, and by the word of their testimony; and they loved not their lives unto the death. (Rev 12:11)*

God has given us power to defeat Him on earth. (Jer 51:20). Jesus already did His own part and gave us victory. He said: "it is finished." Now, we are fighting from victory, not for victory (Rev 12:11). But why don't we see the manifestation of this victory? Why do we see struggle and sometimes it appears as if Satan is winning the battle? The answer to this is because we are not in our rightful place of power and not exercising the authority that Jesus has given us. The Kingdom of God comes in power and must be deliberately demonstrated —by force (Mat 11:12). This is the "violence" of the saints and the only language the kingdom of Satan understands. Are we in this stage of authority let alone the high place of dominion?

We must, however, realize that we are not the one doing the battle, it is the Lord, and we are only His war-clubs (Jer 51:20). Our weapon of warfare is so potent that it stops the enemy dead in his tracks. It is time we began to use this powerful weapon: the **word of our testimony,** to pull down every imagination and every high thing that puffs itself up against the knowledge of God (2Co 10:4-6). This is how Satan wars in the heart of a believer. We must, therefore, bring all thoughts, schemes, plans, intentions, and manipulations of the enemy in our hearts into captivity and obedience of Christ. Our faith-filled words, the words of our testimony, the confession of our lips will achieve this.

However, we cannot effectively do this if we do not first and foremost confess Jesus as Lord.

> *For it is written, As I live, saith the Lord, every knee shall bow to me, and every tongue shall confess to God. (Rom 14:11)*

Without this, all other confessions are powerless and in vain. Jesus is the High Priest of our confession (Heb 3:1). It is when we confess Jesus that our confession can be mighty through God to pull down these strongholds. If we do not confess Jesus, Jesus cannot confess our testimony to the Father. The devil knows the potency and efficacy of this and has moved to reduce the confession and the words of testimony in the mouth of believers to mere words and empty testimony, devoid of power. We must break loose by going back to the basis.

Today, we see and hear a lot of testimony of Jesus around us but there is no commensurate power following. It is because the foundation has been tampered with. The devil has made the foundation through which this is built ineffective. When the foundation is destroyed, there is nothing the righteous can do. The testimony of Jesus is the spirit of prophecy. (Rev 19:10) We must speak forth the victory of Jesus. We must confess it over and over until we see it established. Even though it tarries, we must wait for it.

Mouth and Heart
Confession of the Lord Jesus Christ is the beginning of Salvation.

> *That if thou shalt confess with thy mouth the Lord Jesus, and shalt believe in thine heart that God hath raised him from the dead, thou shalt be saved. (Rom 10:9)*

Many people think to confess is just to agree about the existence of something and affirm it. This is hardly the case. To have this mindset is also to agree about the existence of Satan and his ministry (to steal, to kill and to destroy), yet do nothing about them. Faith is action. We are to resist him by the confession of our mouth.

To confess means not only to tell about His Person but also to demonstrate His power. This is done by speaking the word and watching it become life. Jesus said, "the words that I speak to you they are spirit and they are life." (Joh 6:63) Our words must also be life and take on bodily forms and act as we command. This is when it can overcome. Telling about His work without demonstrating His power is a confession of lips that does not originate from the heart. This is what the last day is all about: all words, no action. The kingdom of

God is given by grace but accessed by action since the time of John the Baptist when there was a shift from the old order.

God said, "let there be light, and there was light." Several times Jesus spoke to those who were sick, and they were healed (Mat 12:13). It means that if we do the same, we will get the same answer. This is because the spoken word is the original seed. God said:

> *So shall my word be that goeth forth out of my mouth: it shall not return unto me void, but it shall accomplish that which I please, and it shall prosper in the thing whereto I sent it. (Isa 55:11)*
>
> *The word of God is quick, and powerful, and sharper than any two-edged sword, piercing to the dividing asunder of soul and spirit, and of the joints and marrow, and is a discerner of the thoughts and intents of the heart. (Heb 4:12)*

There is power in the confessed or spoken word. But it has no power if it abides alone (John 12:24). It has no power if it does not come from the heart. The heart is the root of all things. Whatever the heart believes, the mouth speaks. We must believe in the heart that God will do it, then, our mouth can confess what is believed. We must believe the words of Jesus saying:

> *And whatsoever ye shall ask in my name, that will I do, that the Father may be glorified in the Son. If ye shall ask any thing in my name, I will do it. (Joh 14:13-14)*

Faith Comes From the Heart

> *For verily I say unto you, That whosoever shall say unto this mountain, Be thou removed, and be thou cast into the sea; and shall not doubt in his heart, but shall believe that those things which he saith shall come to pass; he shall have whatsoever he saith. (Mar 11:23)*

Also, it is not enough to just believe in the heart without speaking forth. Because we believe, so we speak. God is looking for those who will actively *decimate* the kingdom of darkness with the confession of their mouths, not just with the thoughts of their head. Our words are commands issued to the host of heaven to war on our behalf. Without the words, there is nothing the principalities will war on. "You shall say to this mountain. ..." Victory is in saying. It is in confessing. There is nothing Satan fears more than the spoken word, backed by faith from the mouth of a believer, it is the original seed. Use it to destroy the kingdom of darkness. Speak it to the air so the prince of the air will be bound. Jesus spoke to the church through Peter:

> *I will give you the keys of the kingdom of heaven, and whatever you bind on earth shall be bound in heaven, and whatever you loose on earth shall be loosed in heaven. (Mat 16:19; 18:18)*

The testimony of our lips or the word of our testimony must be rooted in the belief in our heart that God is faithful to His words and He will do it. The faith-filled words in our mouth and the confession of our lips fulfill the law of life. Our fear-filled words fulfill the law of death. We overcame by the blood of the lamb and the testimony of our mouth. That testimony is rooted in the heart, for whatever the heart believes, the mouth confesses.

Free Will and Choice

> *Rise ye up, take your journey, and pass over the river Arnon: behold, I have given into thine hand Sihon the Amorite, king of Heshbon, and his land: begin to possess it, and contend with him in battle. (Deu 2:24)*

Each time I read the above verse, I always ask myself: "why wouldn't God just fight the whole battle for us and just hand over the complete victory to us?" Maybe you do, too. The answer again is because He always involves us in what He is doing. He wants us to participate in the victory. He wants to prove to the adversary that His son can defeat him. It is not just Him running around for him. We see the vivid example of this with Job. God vouched for Job and gave Satan liberty to try him. He promised him that Job would defeat him without His help, and he did.

A child of God is god and he will have victory as his Father has victory. God calls us to a life of victory. "Because greater is he that is in you than he that is in the world." (1Jn 4:4)

Why would God say that He has given us victory and still want us to go to battle? God has indeed defeated the enemy for us, but He has given us the power and the ability to act on that victory and take possession of it. He will not throw that on our laps. If God did that, we would never learn how to be victors.

Although, man has a free will but it is limited to the choice available to him. Since he possessed a soul, he must use his free will to make choices. If there had been only one tree in the Garden, then, his free will would have been limited to the only choice.

Adam and Eve were still in the pristine state with God before the wrong choice was made. How did they ever make a wrong choice since nothing wrong or evil had entered the Garden? Where did 'wrong' come from?

To answer this is to ask another question about Lucifer, the son of the morning.

> *Thou art the anointed cherub that covereth; and I have set thee so: thou wast upon the holy mountain of God; thou hast walked up and down in the midst of the stones of fire. Thou wast perfect in thy ways from the day that thou wast created, till iniquity was found in thee. (Eze 28:14-15)*

With such staggering credentials with God in heaven as an arch-angel, how did evil enter his heart, where did the "iniquity" that was found in him come from if he was in heaven with God? The testimony we have of heaven is that nothing evil is there.

Perhaps Isaiah 14:3-20 sheds a little light on that but our concern is why Adam and Eve made the wrong choice in the Garden.

When Satan fell from heaven, he appropriated the atmospheric heaven as his domain. He became the prince of this [soul] realm. His title was Baalzebub, meaning the "Lord or owner of the flies." He knows the laws and the operations of the soul. He did not force Adam and Eve to make the choice. He cannot force you to do what you don't want to do but he can pressure you to make a choice. Even at that, you have the power to resist him "and he will flee." (Jas 4:7)

The heart of man is made of both soul and spirit. The spirit is to experience God, and soul is the seat of will, mind, and emotions: to make Adam (and us) fulfill mandate on earth. Satan simply appealed to the soul part of Adam and Eve and pressured them to make a choice. Any choice made in this realm is a wrong choice by default. Today, he does the same. He appeals to the soul and pressures man to make a choice. It is a deceit. He boasts conquest in this realm and that is why we are encouraged to yield to the spirit, only then and only then can we not fulfill the desires (appeal) of the flesh.

God wants His children to know that Satan is not resting; he is on a mission, and we must not seek to rest yet. He wants us to know that a part-time Christian cannot defeat a full-time devil. We must put on the whole armor of God. We must not only begin well, but we must also finish strong. "Jesus said unto him, No man, having put his hand to the plough, and looking back, is fit for the kingdom of God." (Luk 9:62). God expects us not only to begin or come to Him but also to be complete in Him.

> *Beware lest any man spoil you through philosophy and vain deceit, after the tradition of men, after*

> *the rudiments of the world, and not after Christ. For in him dwelleth all the fulness of the Godhead bodily. And ye are complete in him, which is the head of all principality and power. (Col 2:8-10)*

God's pattern of achieving victory for a believer is a process. Maturity comes from starting as a baby and growing up to the full stature: "unto a perfect man, unto the measure of the stature of the fulness of Christ:

> *That we henceforth be no more children, tossed to and fro, and carried about with every wind of doctrine, by the sleight of men, and cunning craftiness, whereby they lie in wait to deceive. (Eph 4:13-14)*

Everything has a process of time. Until we pass through the process and season even in spiritual things, we cannot be proven. God does not use untried and untested vessels. We cannot achieve or demonstrate the victory that God has given us in Christ if we do not pass through the cycle. Jesus passed through the same cycle, and He is our high Priest. "For we have not a high priest which cannot be touched with the feeling of our infirmities; but was in all points tempted like as we are, yet without sin." (Heb 4:15) We only talk the talk but do not demonstrate the power of the talk, or walk the walk. We cannot walk in same power like the early church, and we cannot mature into abundant life which ushers us into eternal life if we do not pass through this cycle. There is no short cut to heaven.

5

DISPENSATION OF REBELLION

"For I bear them record that they have a zeal of God, but not according to knowledge. For they being ignorant of God's righteousness, and going about to establish their own righteousness, have not submitted themselves unto the righteousness of God."
- **Romans 10:2-3**

AS POWER CORRUPTS and absolute power corrupts absolutely, so does freedom. In the spirit realms, there is no absolute freedom. Absolute freedom is sheer lawlessness. How can we be free from the law, and not bound to Christ? How can we be free from sin and not bound to righteousness? (Rom 6:18, 22) Holiness is out of sin, and in to righteousness. How can we claim to abide in grace, yet sin abounds at our doors and altars? (Rom 6:1)

It is the character of man to rebel but the character of God to judge and bring all rebellion into the obedience of Christ (Rom 10:9).

Evil Seed

Satan is the author and the initiator of rebellion. He rebelled from the beginning with his five "I wills." He sews the same seed of rebellion into the hearts of Eve and Adam, too. That is the only thing he had that he could give.

Satan gave his obsession to rebellion to Cain who also rebelled against God by giving God a despicable offering. He later killed his brother, Abel but denied it, and even lied to God's face about Abel's whereabout. When God pronounced the judgment against him, he negotiated his punishment with God…

In Genesis chapter six, we are told how the sons of God also rebelled.

> *The sons of God saw the daughters of men that they were fair; and they took them wives of all which they chose. (Gen 6:2)*

This term in many places in the Old Testament scripture refers to angels (Job 2: 38:7), and if it means the same here, it means that these [evil] angels coveted and lusted after humans, abducted and raped them to produce giant offspring (Nephilims). This is contrary to God's order of reproduction, and also the law of Genesis: every seed reproduces after its own kind.

Earlier, when Satan fell from heaven, he took with him in rebellion against God a third of the angels. Jude also tells about another class of angels who also rebelled with God by leaving their estate:

> *And the angels which kept not their first estate, but left their own habitation, he hath reserved in everlasting chains under darkness unto the judgment of the great day. (Jud 1:6)*

These are different from the previous ones who fell with Satan. While these ones are currently in everlasting chains under darkness until the Day of Judgment, those who fell with Satan are currently on earth now actively working with him.

Satan has consistently use rebellion as a weapon, and he is giving man this benefit. Adam and Eve fell for it. Although they were given free will, they used it wrongly by making the wrong choice in Eden. This is tantamount to rebellion. Consequently, they lost the spirit of God in them. From then onward, the thought and imagination of man's heart (now soul only, spirit being dead) is evil continually. Adam and Eve lost the art of coming to God in worship, walking with Him in fellowship and maturing into Him in sonship.

The Root

If God had given man a choice and freewill as regards his physical make-up just as He gave him freewill in spirit and soul make-up, man would have also rebelled against God with his body. He would have chosen his own sex, height, growth, color, race, family, cycle, etc. But it was just a matter of time for him to know how to do just that, and much more. His devious heart was constantly devising ingenious evil over the ages. It simply reserved the power of grand rebellion to the last age.

Man in the last days has not only played to the gallery in the display of arrogant rebellion against God in his physical make-up, he has also taken it to another level. He can alter, augment or remove any part of the body considered not good enough. He has desecrated the sanctity and institution of marriage which was created and ordained by God to be intimacy between man and woman: it can now be between man and man, woman and woman or even human and beast. This has existed before, at least we read of Sodom and Gomorrah but it is doubtful if they took it to this dimension of altering their sexuality. Today, there is the knowledge to change from one sex to the other at will. It is now becoming normal and acceptable, even in the church. There is enough *Freedom Act* not to judge or discriminate this choice, even in the face of clear biblical instructions (Rom 1:24-29).

Will Sodom and Gomorrah not stand to claim righteousness compared to this generation? Will God lower His standard, knowing that it is not only they which commit such things that are worthy of death, but also those who have pleasure in them that do them. (Rom 1:32)

We are warned:

> *Take heed, brethren, lest there be in any of you an evil heart of unbelief, in departing from the living God. (Heb 3:12)*

When this evil seed of rebellion is sown into a heart, the soul rebels against God cumulatively like Saul until he grieves the Holy Spirit. The result is to depart from God by embracing the thing God already warned to abstain from.

Adam and Eve ate from the tree God already warned them not to eat from. The mediums and witches, which Saul already banished and excommunicated from the land became the oracle where his salvation and deliverance hung. The people that God had warned that Israel should not marry were those who were pleasing to Solomon and Samson. May the power of God break every heart that the seed of rebellion is already growing in Jesus name, especially the church.

Dispensational Rebellion
Despite the faithfulness of God, man still mars each dispensation with utter rebellion.

- First Dispensation: Age of Innocence –From Creation to the Fall. Man chose the fruit of the tree of the knowledge of good and evil over the tree of life.
- Second Dispensation: Age of Conscience - From the Fall to the Flood. Man chose the flood, rather than the ark.
- Third Dispensation: Age of Government – From the Flood to Babel. Nimrod usurped God's authority and stood in the place of God over the people (Gen 10:8-9).
- Fourth Dispensation: Age of the Patriarchs and the Promise – From Abraham to Moses. Through disobedience, Israel went into captivity for four hundred and thirty years.
- Fifth Dispensation: Age of the Law and the Prophets - From Moses to Pentecost. Israel rejected the Messiah.
- Sixth dispensation: the Church Age, the Age of the Gentiles or Age of Grace – From Pentecost to the

Rapture of the Church. The church is rejecting Christ and accessing God through religion instead of Holy Spirit.

Paul described Israel thus:

> *For I bear them record that they have zeal of God, but not according to knowledge. For they, being ignorant of God's righteousness, and going about to establish their own righteousness, have not submitted themselves unto the righteousness of God. (Rom 10:2-3)*

Israel rejected the Father. Judah rejected the Son and now the Church is rejecting the Holy Spirit.

The church has neglected God's righteousness and going about to establish her own righteousness. She has not submitted herself to the righteousness of God. She has institutionalized her own pattern so much that God's normal pattern seems abnormal to a normal Christian who tries to walk the normal pattern.

At this dispensation of the church, the law and the prophets, the instrument of salvation for the immediate previous age (Age of the Law for Israel) can no longer bring us into the fullness of Christ. That instrument existed from Moses UNTIL JOHN:

> *For all the prophets and the law prophesied until John. (Mat 11:13, Luk 16:16)*

From the time of John the Baptist till now, that instrument can no longer save. Jesus instituted a New Testament (Mat. 26:28). He is the Author of a better covenant (Heb 9:15).

A Better Covenant
The disciples are ministers of a New (not old) Testament because the Old Testament was a Testament of death (2Co 3:6). It became obsolete. God is no longer bringing people to His purpose and experience through that covenant because it was testament of death (Rom 7:6).

From the beginning of the New Testament (Pentecost) to the end (Rapture), it is Jesus working through the Holy Spirit. Therefore laws or doctrines of the Old Testament cannot lead the church. But the church today still clings to the practices of the Old Covenant, which is for Israel. She is still energized with and enmeshed in the practices of the previous dispensation, particularly, the practices and operation of the prophets according to the Old Testament order.

Denominations can be built by laws or doctrines, not the church of Jesus Christ. Most 'prophets' today are still the Old Testament-styled prophets, completely oblivious of the functions of the New Testament prophets in the five-fold ministry (Eph 4:11).

Israel and the Church
Another error of the last day church is that she sees herself as the spiritual Israel. Therefore, she does not fully explore and enjoy the newness, benefits, and blessings of the New Covenant. Her practices are still in line with the religion of Israel, which was only provided for the church as a historical

documentation of how God dealt with Israel. The church has failed to realize that she has her own unique calling and dealings.

> *For whatsoever things were written aforetime were written for our learning, that we through patience and comfort of the scriptures might have hope. (Rom 15:4)*

The church is the bride of Christ and Israel is the people of God. They have different and distinct roles in the overall plan of God. The "law and the prophets" was given to Israel but Faith and the Holy Spirit is given to the church. We cannot steal from what God gave to Israel in the expired covenant and use it in the new covenant. It became obsolete because it lost its luster, power, and potency. It could not even be refurbished for reuse but was entirely abolished.

A new covenant was given through Jesus Christ who "…obtained a more excellent ministry, by how much also he is the mediator of a better covenant, which was established upon better promises. For if that first covenant had been faultless, then should no place have been sought for the second." (Heb 8: 6, 7)

The Old Testament writing is to show how God dealt with Israel in the previous dispensation and of course, it is still the scriptures, and useful for our learning.

> *All scripture profitable for doctrine, for reproof, for correction, for instruction in righteousness: That the man of God may be perfect, thoroughly furnished unto all good works. (2Ti 3:16-17)*

If the law and the prophets were still needed, there would have been no need to write a New Testament. John wrote:

> *These are written, that ye might believe that Jesus is the Christ, the Son of God; and that believing ye might have life through his name. (Joh 20:31)*

The New Testament was written to bring life through the name of Jesus, and no longer through the observance of the law of the old. Of course, the old is till useful but to point us to the new, and to let us know why the new is necessary. The Torah was written and in use for thousands of years. But once there was a change in covenant, there was need to write another 'Torah', no longer with the law and prophets but by Faith and the Holy Spirit.

Life and salvation are no longer in the expired covenant but in the new one. The Old Testament is the New Testament concealed, and the New Testament is the Old Testament revealed. To live in the New Covenant but still hold on to 'salvation' or practices of the Old is like putting new wine into an old wine skin (Mar 2:22). The old is for our learning. Now that hope has come, we must allow faith to take over from there.

Since salvation in the New Covenant is by grace through faith in Jesus, not by the observance of the law as it was in the Old Covenant (Eph 2:8-9), we must know that the religion of Israel then is not the same as that of the church of the living God now. Whatever fascination it holds for us must be sacrificed on the altar of faith in Jesus and the power of the Holy Spirit. We cannot return to the old and the abolished practices even if it has its own semblance of piety or structure. The truth is that it is an old 'format,' it has expired.

The Laodecian Church

However, there is so much over-shadowing influence of the Old Covenant in the New Covenant worship, services and practices so much that the end time church has put the Holy Spirit in the passenger seat or reserved list. The elements of the old covenant practices are still strong. One of the reasons for this is because there is cultural resemblance and traditional acceptance. She is navigating the traffic by the instrument of the Old Covenant. She is deceived by growth, but not inner growth; conversion, but not discipleship; power and people's approval, but not God's. Jesus predicted her haughtiness:

> *I know thy works, that thou art neither cold nor hot: I would thou wert cold or hot. So then because thou art lukewarm, and neither cold nor hot, I will spew thee out of my mouth. Because thou sayest, I am rich, and increased with goods, and have need of nothing; and knowest not that thou art wretched, and miserable, and poor, and blind, and naked. (Rev 3:15-18)*

How shall this generation be rescued? Jesus says to her:

> *I counsel thee to buy of me gold tried in the fire, that thou mayest be rich; and white raiment, that thou mayest be clothed, and that the shame of thy nakedness do not appear; and anoint thine eyes with eyesalve, that thou mayest see. (Rev 3:15-18)*

If God could open the eyes of Hagar to see the provision around her so she and her son would be sustained and not die in the wilderness, He can do much more for the church only if she comes in faith and humility. As Hagar departed from Sarah, so also the church must depart from Israel. God's plan for both are different.

God wants us to be part of what He is doing now, yet He will not lower His standard. Grace, through faith and the Holy Spirit is the only way given at this age to come to the Father. All the previous ways were but shadows of The Way. Jesus affirmed:

> *I am the way, the truth, and the life: no man cometh unto the Father, but by me. (Joh 14:6)*

But people were, and are still so much attached to the shadow that when the real came, they found it too vivid, convicting and non-conforming to their age-long traditions.

Jesus challenged Judah on these traditions, He asked them why they make "the word of God of none effect through your traditions, which ye have delivered: and many such like things do ye…" (Mar 7:13). Paul also warned:

> *Beware lest any man spoil you through philosophy and vain deceit, after the tradition of men, after the rudiments of the world, and not after Christ. (Col 2:8)*

Just as Judah embraced traditions, the church is embracing philosophy rather than faith, program rather than a process, religion rather than relationship and system rather than a Person.

Foundational Defects
In his time, Paul wept to see what many had replaced Christianity with. He cried:

> *For many walk, of whom I have told you often, and now tell you even weeping, that they are the enemies of the cross of Christ... (Phi 3:18)*

There are many good walks but not God-walk. There are Christian walks but not Christ-walk. There are many walks, but not according to pattern. Paul stated their aim and their glory and also predicted their end: "...whose end is destruction."

Paul told us that the reason why many did not walk according to pattern is because of "their belly", "vain glory" and "earthly things." These reasons haven't changed much with today's church. Many cause divisions and offenses in the gathering in order to establish their own pattern, denomination, institution, ministry, and empire. They sustain membership by strange doctrines, traditions, and ritualistic practices. They indirectly become the Holy Spirit to the congregation.

The so-called prophets give direction in the Old Covenant order, and much of the body ministry are ritualistic and align more with the Mosaic temple worship of rituals, observance, performance et al, than worshipping in spirit and in truth. This is sadly, more of a leadership issue. Everyone coming in simply follows the established and age-long pattern, changing a few things to personalize it without individually coming to God in faith, like the Berean Christians, to know what God is calling them to do. Those who come into the ministry on this platform are thus initiated into a wrong order right from the beginning, and the cycle continues. If the foundation is destroyed, what can the righteous do?

Many believers have sincerely grown to believe that gospel message is about rhetoric, motivational messages, "excellence of speech and enticing words of man's wisdom," poetic rendition, use and alignment of words to amuse the ears of the hearers. But it is hardly so. Others think the Gospel is miracles, healing, prosperity, breakthrough, fame, etc. It is rather the "demonstration of the spirit and of the power of God, "that your faith should not stand in the wisdom of men, but in the power of God." (1Co 2:5) Such are mystified when they are confronted with the true gospel. They will not be able to endure it because they did not come through that avenue. What is used to bring people into the church must be used to sustain them in the church. If it is music, doctrine, fables, positive confession, motivational talk, message that scintillate the ears, with an appeal to the soul but do not edify the spirit and so on, it will take a miracle for such to know the true gospel. These and those who follow systems, traditions, denominations and doctrines will eventually "shipwreck." (1Ti 1:19) Paul said:

> *Mark them which cause divisions and offences contrary to the doctrine which ye have learned; and avoid them. For they that are such serve not*

> *our Lord Jesus Christ, but their own belly; and by good words and fair speeches deceive the hearts of the simple. (Rom 16:17-18)*

As true believers in the last days, we must be ready to "war a good warfare," and engage in "the battle of faith" in order to be on course with the Lord. The warning of the 'falling away" is for the saints, "those who think that they stand." (1Co 10:12)

There was never a time that believers are prone to bow to the pressure and appeal of social Christianity than this time. Many programs are carefully and irresistibly tailored to offer a sense of religious belonging, activities and solidarity among members. It will leave people in a cyclical rendezvous of just a part but not the full experience of Christ. God wants us to experience the fullness of Him so that we can walk in power, but the enemy will do everything to short-change us.

Why must we rejoice in the experience of just a part of God when provision has been made to enter into His fullness? This is a deceit of the devil: half-truth is more deceitful and deceptive than pure lies. This is the strategy Satan used against Adam and Eve in the Garden: "has God said?" He has no new tricks.

> *Many shall follow their pernicious ways; by reason of whom the way of truth shall be evil spoken of. And through covetousness shall they with feigned words make merchandise of you: whose judgment now of a long time lingereth not, and their damnation slumbereth not. (2Pe 2:2-3)*

It is true that many will be deceived and fall into his hands but we don't have to be part of them. The only way to ensure this is to "resist the devil and he will flee." (Mar 13:5, Luk 21:8, Eph 5:6, 2Th 2:3)

True Christianity does not necessarily follow the pattern of the organized church with its system, yet there is a [spiritual] pattern, which when adhered to, will deliver the same firepower as that of the early church and the disciples. Jesus said greater works than He did we would do. We have not even done anything close to what He did, let alone greater. He will do what He promised to do but we must press in into the provision. Paul told Timothy to walk according to the pattern by which he received Christ: this will help him to war and defeat the adversary. It would help him to hold the faith, have a good conscience, which is necessary for victory. He went further to say:

> *Which some having put away concerning the faith have made shipwreck: Of whom is Hymenaeus and Alexander; whom I have delivered unto Satan, that they may learn not to blaspheme. (1Ti 1:18-20)*

This charge and the warning are for every Christian today who wants to have a normal walk with God through His Son.

This is how we can be a part of building a habitation of God and the church of Jesus and not building personal empire, mere doctrine, religion and tradition of men. We are the materials that Christ will use to build His church, and pull down the church being built by men. We are lively stones, to build a "spiritual house and a holy priesthood, so that you may offer spiritual sacrifices that are acceptable to God through Jesus, the Messiah." (1Pe 2:5)

Let us persuade men to thirst after the fullness of God so that we can enter into the complete cycle of the Christian faith walk and not just recycle a part of it.

For instance, coming to Christ, which is the first step and the spiritual birth of the new believer into the kingdom has been so much recycled that it is presented as all that a believer needs in the new life as a Christian. Many are stuck in this cycle and only relish this one and only experience. However, it is just the beginning of the new life in Christ, there is yet a walk, and that also is by no means the end.

The early disciples experienced all the stages of the Christian life. That is the secret of their success. It is time to rediscover this secret. The secret of the Lord is with those who fear Him. If you fear the Lord and desire to walk in the totality and the fullness of God's provision, it's time to explore the fundamental principles of the doctrine of Christ. Jesus died for one thing:

> *That he might present it to himself a glorious church, not having spot, or wrinkle, or any such thing; but that it should be holy and without blemish. (Eph 5:27)*

The full price of this was paid for. It is time to take what rightfully belongs to us, that Christ may be glorified not just in a part but in all our life.

We have received, not the spirit of the world, but the spirit which is of God; that we might know the things that are freely given to us of God.
(1Co 2:12)

The second section describes in detail the fundamental principles, and the step-by-step process of salvation: the new birth, the new life, the abundant life, leading to eternal life with Christ in heaven.

SECTION II

Therefore leaving the principles of the doctrine of Christ,
let us go on unto perfection; not laying again the
foundation of repentance from dead works,
and of faith toward God, of the doctrine
of baptisms, and of resurrection
of the dead, and of eternal
judgment. And this will
we do, if God permit.
Hebrews 6:1-3

6

BIRTH

"There is joy in heaven over a sinner that repents."
- John 15:7

The New Birth

IS THE NEW birth experience the same thing as salvation?

The doctrine of salvation has puzzled both theologians as well as believers over the centuries. The debate, however, is more pronounced within the Arminianists' and Calvinists' camp.

Summarily, the former holds the view that salvation entirely depends on God for a believer. The latter holds that man has a free will and has a part to play in salvation. The Universalists believe that all will be saved, regardless. Yet, there are other liberals and conservative Christians who hold different points of view, rationalizing all these. But the best point of view is to free ourselves from all man-made doctrines and allow scriptures to interpret scriptures with the witness of the Holy Spirit in our hearts.

We know that law (doctrine) is good if it is used 'lawfully,' but otherwise, it blinds, binds and kills, but the Spirit gives life. We will all stand individually (not denominationally) before God to answer to our beliefs. So, it is imperative for everyone to hold the truth as revealed in our hearts by the Holy Spirit and not by any system of man.

Unlike the Charismatic movement, the Pentecostal lays much emphasis on speaking in "tongues" as the evidence of the new birth. They further hold that the new birth itself occurs when you "give your life to Christ," and that is when you are saved.

This is true in theory but entails much more in practice. It is not what is "received" at the moment that determines salvation, but what that which is received is allowed to accomplish in the life of the recipient. One is the new birth while the other is salvation. The passage below explains it more:

> *And be not conformed to this world: but be ye transformed by the renewing of your mind, that ye may prove what is that good, and acceptable, and perfect, will of God. (Rom 12:2)*

It is the renewing of the mind that transforms believer from the new birth experience to the salvation experience, and this has to be "proven." The verse completes it thus: "that ye may prove what is that good, and acceptable, and perfect, will of God." Although God desires all men to have the new birth, but Salvation is the good, acceptable, and perfect will of God. He desires all to come to the salvation experience. Alas! Not all that experience the new birth goes to experience this. It is a process of renewal and transformation to perfection.

> *He that believeth and is baptized shall be saved. (Mar 16:16)*

In the above passage, it is clear that salvation occurs when a man believes and is baptized. We will examine what to believe and to be baptized mean in the next chapter. These two words are the ingredients of salvation. They are the major "components" of the "basic principles" of becoming a Christian.

The new birth is thus the first step in the overall experience of salvation, just like the physical birth is the beginning of a new life. If it is the beginning, then we can consider the words of the preacher about the beginning of a thing:

> *Better is the end of a thing than the beginning thereof: and the patient in spirit is better than the proud in spirit. (Ecc 7:8)*

It is not a good thing, but it is common to begin the Christian journey and not proceed further. It is a misconception and a (theological) tragedy to believe or assume that the beginning is the same as the end. It is better not to begin at all: for God hates the backsliders (Ecc 5:5, Heb 10:38-39)

The beginning of a thing may be good but it is not all that begins well that ends well, the new birth experience inclusive. It is only when we stay the course to the end that the beginning is worthwhile.

In the words of the writer of the book of Hebrews:

> *For we are made partakers of Christ, if we hold the beginning of our confidence steadfast unto the end. (Heb 3:14)*

In the Christian journey, many truly begin well and enter through the right way, but not all continue to the end. Paul asked believers in the church of Galatia:

> *Ye did run well; who did hinder you that ye should not obey the truth? (Gal 5:7)*

This means that it is possible to be hindered from the race after it commenced well. What keeps believers going to the end is when he keeps obeying "the truth." The beginning is good but the blessing (salvation) is in the end. Thus, contrary to many beliefs and teachings, being made partakers of Christ (salvation) is dependent on holding the BEGINNING of our confidence (new birth) to the END. Salvation is not gotten at the beginning but at the end:

> *He that endureth to the end shall be saved. (Mat 10:22)*

So, we see that to end well is as important as to begin well. To achieve this is not by observing some set of rules or doctrines of men about what salvation is and what it is not. It is to trust that the same power that brought us in will keep us through, and to the end.

The end can be few hours after the new birth. It can be months or years, or even decades. The time is not as important as the process. It is the quality of life during this journey that matters. It has to be in the power of the Holy

Spirit not by the struggles of flesh, or the observance and belief of a doctrine. It is faith walk with the person of Jesus not with theologians, past or present 'reformers.' It is not even with a movement, denomination or any religious personality but Jesus alone *(Sola Christo)*.

The Life Cycle

An adage says that it takes two to tango. In the same vein, birth does not just occur on its own. The Oxford dictionary defines birth as:

> *The emergence of a baby or other young from the body of its mother; the start of life as a physically separate being.* [ii]

From this, it is obvious that every birth requires a mother, and sometimes, a midwife to perform the 'delivery' or separate the young life from its mother.

The cycle of life in the physical is precipitated by a biological life inside the womb, which passes through a gestation period. The same is applicable in the spiritual. Since life today is an extension of the seed of yesterday, it means that we are all extension of life from Eden. We were in the loins of Adam. If he succeeded, we succeed, if he failed, we fail but the latter was the reality. When he died, we died with him (Heb 7).

When Adam and Eve died, the process of spiritual gestation was aborted. This was because we were in their loins, we died with them. David said:

> *Behold, I was shapen in iniquity; and in sin did my mother conceive me. (Psa 51:5)*

So, when a child is born into the world, though he has not yet committed sin in the context of what we know sin as, but the truth is that he was actually born in sin, he or she is a sinner and needs redemption even as a baby. This is a truth we have to know so that the concept of our needing redemption becomes clearer. We do not need redemption because of the sins we are committing now, but rather, we need redemption because of the sin of Adam, which is imputed unto the whole of human race: "For all have sinned, and come short of the glory of God." (Rom 3:23) We all sinned with Adam and we all died with him.

However, we were also in the loins of Jesus, the second Adam. Satan did attempt to kill Jesus as he did Adam and Eve but he failed. Consequently, we were not aborted in Jesus as were in Adam. This is because Jesus resurrected, we also resurrected with Him and in Him. We can see that our life is hinged on the first and the second Adam. There is no salvation in any other place except these two. We died in the first Adam, we live in the second Adam. Any other "Adam" is a counterfeit.

> *For as in Adam all die, even so in Christ shall all be made alive. (1Co 15:22)*

Thus, death in Adam in the Garden was restored to life in Christ in Calvary. At the normal gestation period in the spirit, life is birthed into the kingdom to begin to experience the very life God wanted for Adam and Eve at the beginning.

As we can see, both physical birth and spiritual birth are followed by life. However, the physical life proceeds to death in its normal cycle, but spiritual life does not, rather, it proceeds to abundant life (Joh 10:10). In the new life, death is completely swallowed. That is why we can boldly say:

> *O death, where is thy sting? O grave, where is thy victory? The sting of death is sin; and the strength of sin is the law. But thanks be to God, which giveth us the victory through our Lord Jesus Christ. (1Co 15:55-57)*

Abundant life is the spiritual substitute for death in the physical. If you want abundant life, it is only in Christ. It swallows up death. That is why if you know the Son, the second Adam, you can never die again. Because He lives forever, you will also live forever. To those, physical death is a window to eternal life. It is something to long and look forward to with joy and hope. Paul said:

> "*For to me to live is Christ, and to die is gain.*" *(Phi 1:21)*

Can you say that of your self? The fear of death is gone. Paul describes this victory further:

> *For we know that if our earthly house of this tabernacle were dissolved, we have a building of God, an house not made with hands, eternal in the heavens. For in this we groan, earnestly desiring to be clothed upon with our house which is from heaven: If so be that being clothed we shall not be found naked. For we that are in this tabernacle do groan, being burdened:not for that we would be unclothed, but clothed upon, that*

> *mortality might be swallowed up of life. Now he that hath wrought us for the selfsame thing is God, who also hath given unto us the earnest of the Spirit. Therefore we are always confident, knowing that, whilst we are at home in the body, we are absent from the Lord: (For we walk by faith, not by sight:) We are confident, I say, and willing rather to be absent from the body, and to be present with the Lord. Wherefore we labour, that, whether present or absent, we may be accepted of him. (2Co 5:1-9)*

This is consistent with the mission statement of Jesus in John 10:10:

> *I am come that they might have life, and that they might have it more abundantly.*

Please, note that when this spiritual birth occurs, it means that a young life is born into the spirit, and it is to experience a new life in the new kingdom and grow to maturity. What just happened is a 180 degrees turn-around from the way of death to the way of life. The journey of life in the new kingdom has just begun. It will be lived by the help and power of the Holy Spirit in the believer, which is received during this process.

This new birth, which just occurs proceeds to other experiences like the baptisms, fellowship and so on. The completion of these experiences which are by the faith in Jesus and the working of the Holy Spirit received at this time culminate in salvation, which in turn leads to eternal life.

This is the normal Christian cycle. Have you experienced the first step into all these experiences – the new birth? If you have, you have begun the journey into the kingdom. This journey is called the walk of faith.

> *As ye have therefore received Christ Jesus the Lord, so walk ye in him: Rooted and built up in him, and stablished in the faith, as ye have been taught, abounding therein with thanksgiving. Beware lest any man spoil you through philosophy and vain deceit, after the tradition of men, after the rudiments of the world, and not after Christ. For in him dwelleth all the fulness of the Godhead bodily. (Col 2:6-9)*

The Midwife

As already said, birth is the very first step to experience life, both physical and spiritual. The physical culminates in death while the spiritual culminates in abundant life here on earth, which in turn leads into eternal life in heaven.

When birth occurs, and a child is born (again), many parameters have to be examined to determine if there is life in the birth. This is because there are many births without life. One of the parameters is the midwife or delivery system. This is because no birth or delivery is the same. While some are quite normal, some are painful, while others are grotesque, barbaric and or cruel. These factors determine the mortality rate.

My father once told me that his mother had seven births, but he was the only one that survived. Which means that although there were seven births, but only one life. The same is applicable in the spirit: there are many births, but few lives in Christ. Christ is interested in life. He died so that we may live. So the new birth (born again) should not be seen as salvation.

I thought my father's situation was alarming until I heard from another person that his grandmother had seventeen births but only his father survived! Almost every home in Africa or other parts of the world at one time or the other in the past experienced this. It accounted for high mortality rate in those regions at that time.

Many other factors were responsible for this but we cannot examine them here. Today however, there is improvement in the delivery and the midwifery system and this has led to a decrease in the mortality rate, and of course, population explosion. Although my father survived, he still followed the normal cycle of physical life, which is death, just like every human being in the cycle of time. But to those who survived [spiritual] birth and proceeds to abundant life, there is no death, but eternal life.

There is definitely a rejoicing with every birth of normal delivery, both physical and spiritual. Jesus said there is joy in heaven over every sinner that repents. (Joh 15:7) This is for a normal Christian delivery. We shall examine the topic of repentance in much detail in subsequent chapters.

Some deliveries have complications in one way or the other and can be said to be abnormal. Some are stillbirths, but birth, anyway. Some are with life-threatening and life-altering complications. Some have short lives, only experiencing life for a period and then expire.

Similarly, many do survive the initial birth, but do not grow into maturity for no fault of theirs. Parental neglect, lack of experience and [hyper] love account for some of the reasons for this. Other reasons could be fear of losing the baby, fear of falling or being injured during the process of learning to stand and to walk, or just fear of being alone. Where there is fear, there cannot be fulfillment because fear is of the devil. He comes to steal, to kill and to destroy.

However, it is appalling that some parents would deliberately want to make their children perpetual babies in order to serve their benefits and purposes. Some do it for commercial gains, making merchandise of parenthood. These are those who milk the sheep rather than feed them. Paul called them "enemies of the cross of Christ: Whose end is destruction, whose God is their belly, and whose glory is in their shame, who mind earthly things." (Php 3:18-19)

Rather than to give babies the sincere milk of the word so that they can grow, they feed them with vain words (Eph 5:6), enticing words (1Cor 2:4, Col 2:4), "philosophy and vain deceit, after the tradition of men, after the rudiments of the world, and not after Christ." (Col 2:8)

Sadly, such babes never grow to understand the spiritual reason for their living, other than to be "successful in life and, or ministry." Undoubtedly, they *gave their lives to Christ* at one time or the other, they are sincere with God and qualified to be called "virgins." But like the virgins in the parable of the ten virgins, they lack the oil (Holy Spirit). Consequently, they cannot see (the things of the spirit), for the Holy Spirit is the lamp that lights the path. Although, these people have life, but the life they have does not lead to abundant life. They grope in darkness (lack of understanding of spiritual things), only USING the name of Jesus to achieve personal benefits and mundane things. They are still "virgins," only that they lack the oil –the quickening power that will set their hearts on alert and prepared for the groom's arrival is not there. When the bridegroom finally comes, although these virgins wake up from slumber like the rest of the virgins, but since there is no oil in their lamp to light their way, they cannot meet the bridegroom. In the same vein, those who fall into this category of believers cannot progress to eternal life with Christ. That is why they are referred to as the foolish virgins.

> *Then they also which are fallen asleep in Christ are perished. If in this life only we have hope in Christ, we are of all men most miserable.*
> *(1Co 15:18-19)*

Another angle to this is that the life of those who fall into this category is doctored by their [spiritual] "parents." Many of the so-called "father-in-the-Lord" ignorantly or ambitiously 'use them' to achieve their own ministerial goals. They make such person a member or even official in their ministry, organization or denomination rather than the body of Christ. The development and commitment of such sincere Christian is thus rooted in works, zeal and performance for God through those avenues. This is the "faith walk" they know, proud of and faithful with. How terrible it is to be under a wrong anointing or spiritual parent.

But God will not keep sincere believers who fall victim of this too long in such places. He will not abandon anyone with a sincere heart for Him. One day, the thirst for more of God will consume them. The hunger will lead them out and separate them from any denomination or organized religious setting they may be stranded in. They will hear the inner voice saying:

> *Come out from among them, and be ye separate, saith the Lord, and touch not the unclean thing; and I will receive you, And will be a Father unto you, and ye shall be my sons and daughters, saith the Lord Almighty. (2Co 6:17-18)*

They will hear the voice of God calling: "where art thou" or "get thee out of thy country, and from thy kindred, and from thy father's house, unto a land that I will shew thee..." (Gen 12:1)

When this happens, no attraction provided by such organization will tie them down.

> *Verily, verily, I say unto you, The hour is coming, and now is, when the dead shall hear the voice of the Son of God: and they that hear shall live. (Joh 5:25)*

Salvation

Many begin their journey of spiritual life at crusades, revival meetings, and mission fields or other gatherings. Those who respond to the "altar calls" are prayed for. They are made to recite the 'sinners' prayer' and then pronounced "saved." This is an erroneous Gospel, if to call it a gospel at all.

Although the process is right, but it simply means the person has begun the process of salvation but not saved yet. Salvation is a gift conferred on you by God, not any preacher. It is much the same as someone who just enrolled to study a course in a college. He has been admitted into the school and the purpose is to study. Certificate of Graduation is conferred on successful completion of the course, not at enrolment. It is much the same in the spiritual: it is God that confers salvation on believers "upon successful completion" of the process (not program) of faith walk, which is only by the power of the Holy Spirit.

> *And I am sure of this, that he who began a good work in you will bring it to completion at the day of Jesus Christ. (Php 1:6ESV)*

It is he who begins the work that will finish it in the same way. Who or what begins your faith walk: is it the preacher or by yourself or the Holy Spirit? Is it by works or by faith? It is he who begins it that will complete it. Paul said to the Galatian Church:

> *This only would I learn of you, Received ye the Spirit by the works of the law, or by the hearing of faith? Are ye so foolish? having begun in the Spirit, are ye now made perfect by the flesh? (Gal 3:2-3)*

So when a new birth occurs, it is to lead young believer to a [faith] walk with Christ. As the believer walks with Christ, the process of salvation like baptisms, and so on are completed by the Holy Spirit in him and leads him to the completion of what is begun.

Many spiritual births occur daily, but how many of such lead to this walk with Jesus (life), let alone abundant life? How then, can there be eternal life? Many new believers are not introduced to this walk. Their birth becomes static, awkward, doubtful and full of struggles. The spiritual development is stunted and arrested. They remain in this stage, claiming to be saved but without the fruits, gifts or the power of the Spirit.

Some are introduced to this walk "by the works of the flesh," not by the walk of faith and the power of the Holy Spirit who achieves this. They are enmeshed in activities and services. They are into good works, charity and strict denials or observance of certain rules. While these are not wrong by themselves, they are sadly, not the faith walk.

Zacchaeus was a good example of someone who had an encounter with Jesus. He displayed good works:

> *Zacchaeus stood, and said unto the Lord; Behold, Lord, the half of my goods I give to the poor; and if I have taken any thing from any man by false accusation, I restore him fourfold. (Luk 19:8)*

This is a very good state of heart in Zacchaeus. It is a confirmation of his true conviction of who Jesus was. When we have encounter with Jesus, this is bound to happen. If you did not experience this, you will have to look into your coming to Christ again, lest you have believed another Jesus. He works through His Spirit in our hearts. There is a necessity that He convicts us of our past deeds. This is Godly sorrow and leads to repentance.

Some people have argued that when Zacchaeus did that, he was saved because Jesus said to him almost immediately:

> *And Jesus said unto him, This day is salvation come to this house, forsomuch as he also is a son of Abraham. For the Son of man is come to seek and to save that which was lost. (Luk 19:9-10)*

Notice that this was the dispensation of the law. Few people who belonged to that dispensation came to Jesus through other means than the law, and Zacchaeus was one of them. The rich young ruler almost did, too. All anyone needed to do to cross from that dispensation was to believe that Jesus was the Messiah. But the real instrument of salvation for that dispensation was to keep the law. But as many as believed Jesus in that dispensation, Jesus brought them in to the new dispensation.

Another great example of that is also the thief in the right hand of Jesus. His salvation was also instant.

> *And Jesus said unto him, Verily I say unto thee, Today shalt thou be with me in paradise. (Luk 23:43)*

Look again at what Jesus said to Zaccheaus: "… forsomuch as he also is a son of Abraham. For the Son of man is come to seek and to save that which was lost." He was the son Abraham, a Jew. Which means he naturally belonged to a different salvation plan, which was for the Jews. But any Jew who believes in Jesus is brought in, even till today.

Notice also that Jesus said he came to seek and save that which was lost. That was the exclusive mission of Jesus in His earthly life. When He sent out His disciples, He instructed them to go only to the Jews, and not the Gentiles or any other people (Mat 10:5-7). So, all anyone needed in the time of Jesus to be saved was to either keep the law or believe that Jesus was the Messiah. But right now in the dispensation of the church, salvation is not by works of the law, it is a gift of God through faith as we believe Jesus and we are baptized. Believing is coming to Him and being baptized (water, spirit, and fire) is walking with Him.

Paul was so mad with the believers in Galatia and screamed:

> *O foolish Galatians, who hath bewitched you, that ye should not obey the truth, before whose eyes Jesus Christ hath been evidently set forth, crucified among you? (Gal 3:1)*

It is a "bewitchment" at best to introduce believers to a faith walk of performance or to present faith walk to them as to be earned through their own effort in trying to please God by what we do for Him. This is "not obeying the truth" but obeying denominational laws, facts, creeds, religious activities or rituals. It is presenting a striving to make people to see and accept you as a Christian. It is making effort to please God. The things of the spirit are spirits. We cannot please God by works, effort or performance. Zechariah the prophet says:

> *Not by might, nor by power, but by my spirit, saith the LORD of hosts. (Zec 4:6)*

> *...For by strength shall no man prevail. (1Sam 2:9)*

God is ultimately looking for disciple in every convert. While it is good to make coverts, it is important they become disciples. The danger is that many converts may never progress to the stage of life (discipleship).

The command is to go into all the world and "make disciples" of all nations, not converts (Mar 16:15). It is important that preachers properly initiate believers into the normal Christian life through a birth and then a walk of faith. The birth is to <u>come</u> to Christ and the life is to <u>walk</u> with Christ. It is not to entice or lure people into our fantastic programs, life changing [carnal] seminars or beautiful churches. If we do not spell out the spiritual process properly, we will end up with a bunch of coverts who never mature into disciples.

God wants us to come to Him through Jesus, but He also wants us to walk with Him by His Spirit in us, which we receive. It is the Spirit that will lead us into abundant life, which is the door to eternal life. Christ desires that Christians come to all, not just a part of His fullness.

Ministry

We become newborn babes in the Spirit the moment we "believe." It is the beginning of a new start in life. Do not forget that this "belief" is much more than we think it is. You will read more of this in the next chapter.

Babies are terrific sight to behold, but we cannot keep them as babies forever. They must be nurtured to maturity and returned to the Lord (1Sa 1:22) to fulfill the purpose why they are born.

Souls are born [again] into the kingdom in order to follow Christ and to be His representative on earth. Although it is an honor for a servant to be like his master, but Christianity is not an apprenticeship scheme or program where we imitate or mimic leaders so that we be like them. They did not save us and they will not reward us in heaven. We do not follow them but Christ in them. Paul said, "Be ye followers of me, even as I also am of Christ." (1Co 11:1)

We are also called to demonstrate the kingdom of God on earth by the type of life we live, which is strange to the world. This is only possible by the Spirit of God in us. This life will attract people to us. It will also make the world to know that there is a supernatural life they can live but with the power of the Spirit of Christ in them. This is called ministry.

In his book, Ministry, Gordon Gentry explains:

> *In the church, ministries are given to bring us to the unity of the faith, functioning as a body, with each member moving according to the ability God gives. To move in God, each must be spiritually equipped, and that equipment comes from the ability of the Holy Spirit in the lives of the ministers in any local gathering. Ministry is the work of God in the midst of His children for the perfecting (maturing) of the saints. It is for one purpose: the supply of Christ to the body. Ministers are to move in their ministry by the*

> *Spirit until we all are experiencing the fullness of what God wants for us.* [iii]

So, we see that ministry is not when we rent a facility and populate it with people or furniture and put a signpost outside to bring people in. It is not when we register with the government about our activities and services. It is not when we do great works for God. It is simply what you do with the new life in you and the Spirit of God in you with the people around you.

When we approach ministry with a mindset of a corporate body or organization, it gives a false and different mentality. This defeats the individuality of the spirit of Christianity. Christianity is about a person; it is organic in nature but not an organization or religion. Jesus went about doing good… He did not have a headquarter somewhere where He taught and organized services. It is the fragrance of God that came out of His life as He lived that was His ministry, and that should be ours, too. Our ministry is not separate from us.

As you are busy living the life of Christ that is in you through His Spirit, Christ Himself will direct your life for His purpose and glory. You will be able to heal the sick, preach deliverance to those who are bound, bring people to Christ and so on, with results. This is ministry. It is Christ working in you, to will and to do His good pleasure (Php 2:13). It is not something learned in theological school. It is not an intellectual thing. It is the Holy Spirit's ability, which He has given to you. It is the grace in your life that is flowing naturally and effortlessly in your day-to-day life, seen by people around you and it is a blessing to them.

Regardless of how big and enormous such grace flowing out of our lives may be, the only thing worthy of rejoicing on is that our names are written in the book of life (Luk 10:22). We are not to build a movement, organization or empire round it with the mentality "to preserve the true doctrine." God knows how to preserve His works by Himself without your help. If He does not, Christianity would have been long dead and forgotten before you were born and you would not have been a Christian. God is able to do what He wills to do if you will let Him.

Do not let the sincere quest to preserve a supposed *pure* doctrine among people lead you to building an empire or organization round the grace of God in your life. It is a trap of the devil to build "something for God." Consistently throughout church history, once any group led by the Holy Spirit becomes organized, the Holy Spirit leaves to begin a new thing somewhere or with someone else. This is because we cannot 'box' the Holy Spirit. Although the work can still survive and be active for many centuries after, but it's an old glory because God will not repatriate His gifts or calling from whomever He has given, until it naturally wanes out; "the gifts and the calling of God are without repentance." (Rom 11:29)

God brings you in to the kingdom primarily and ultimately to keep you to Himself. Ministry is secondary. Do not let secondary assignment defeat your primary assignment. Eternal life, not ministry must be your priority. Every zeal you have for the Lord about the lost must be with this knowledge. Do not be like Israel who had zeal for God but without knowledge. (Rom 10:2) Zeal eats up. Your eternity supersedes your ministry. You may succeed in ministry and lose eternity. To what then will your reward and labor amount to? Many have taken ministry personal. Paul said:

> *I therefore so run, not as uncertainly; so fight I, not as one that beateth the air: But I keep under my body, and bring it into subjection: lest that by any means, when I have preached to others, I myself should be a castaway. (1Co 9:26-27)*

This is a possibility that we have to guard against. God is more interested in our lives than in our ministry. Ministry is His. If we fail in ministry or refuse to do it, He will always raise someone else, but your life has no replacement. Your personal relationship with God should be of more importance to you than your ministry to the people. In the end, the people may be saved while you miss out.

While God is preparing you for eternity in heaven, He occupies you with ministry here on earth, but He saved you in order to take you home with Him, so that where He is, you will also be in eternity.

> *For what shall it profit a man, if he shall gain the whole world, and lose his own soul? Or what shall a man give in exchange for his soul? (Mar 8:36-37)*

Know that you are dispensable. Don't let zeal for God and for the lost blind your eyes. God is a God of order. This is always a challenge to people who have the call. Prophet Elijah said to God:

> *Lord, they have killed thy prophets, and digged down thine altars; and I am left alone, and they seek my life. But what saith the answer of God unto him? I have reserved to myself seven thousand men, who have not bowed the knee to the image of Baal. (Rom 11:3-4)*

God always have thousands of people who will do better than you. If you die of zeal, God will continue His work but you will have to face Him. You might be saved, but what about your work? Only what we give to God in obedience will survive the fire.

> *According to the grace of God which is given unto me, as a wise masterbuilder, I have laid the foundation, and another buildeth thereon. But let every man take heed how he buildeth thereupon. For other foundation can no man lay than that is laid, which is Jesus Christ. Now if any man build upon this foundation gold, silver, precious stones, wood, hay, stubble. Every man's work shall be made manifest: for the day shall declare it, because it shall be revealed by fire; and the fire shall try every man's work of what sort it is. If any man's work abide which he hath built thereupon, he shall receive a reward. If any man's work shall be burned, he shall suffer loss: but he himself shall be saved; yet so as by fire. (1Co 3: 10-15)*

His work in your life is His ministry in you; it is not your work for Him. Your work for Him, which many call ministry is just your effort. It is only what He enables you to do and gives grace in the same that is ministry to Him.

To Show Forth
We just talked about the fact that God's primary reason for calling us is so that we can reign with Him in eternity. But before eternity comes, He makes us occupied here on earth (Luk 19:13). He makes us to live His life on earth for people to see that He has truly conquered the world. As we do this by His Spirit in us, our light shines to the world and draw souls to the Lord. This is ministry.

> *Ye are the light of the world. A city that is set on an hill cannot be hid. (Mat 5:14)*

Another reason why God called us is to change us from ordinary people to extraordinary people. We are a "peculiar people." He changes us from a gentile nation without God, to a "holy nation in God;" from a wicked and perverse generation to a "chosen generation."

Why did He do these?

> *To shew forth the praises of him who hath called you out of darkness into his marvelous light: Which in time past were not a people, but are now the people of God: which had not obtained mercy, but now have obtained mercy. (1Pe 2:9-10)*

The earth must be full of the glory, praise and power of God, and we are the people to make this happen. We are the epistles that the world reads. This is the mandate of the believer. It is to testify with boldness of God's love, power and saving grace. Believers must demonstrate this so that the world may know that there is a generation of people who are redeemed by the blood of the Lamb from sin, Satan and the world.

When we experience birth, we have crossed from darkness to the light that dispels the darkness. As children of light, we must, therefore, shine this light for the world to see. The book of Proverbs says that the path of the just is as the shining light, that shines more and more unto the perfect day (Pro 4:18). Jesus said:

> *Let your light so shine before men, that they may see your good works, and glorify your Father which is in heaven. (Mat 5:16)*

The question is if we are the light of the world, why is the world still in darkness?

> *The earnest expectation of the creature waiteth for the manifestation of the sons of God. (Rom 8:19)*

At the new birth, the Holy Spirit also changes our focus and orientation from ourself to Himself, and from this world to heaven. Although, we live in the world, but we no longer care for the things of the world. All we want to do is to please Him in worship and to let the world know Him. We are changed from in to out, and then, from glory to glory. We can gladly say: "the things I used to do, I do them no more." We have passed from darkness to God's marvelous light. We can no longer have fellowship with the unfruitful works of darkness, but to reprove them, for it is a shame even to speak of those things which are done of them in secret. (Eph 5:11-12)

Therefore as believers that have experienced the new birth, it is time to "arise and shine," for thy light is come, and the glory of the Lord is risen upon us. (Isa 60:1)

> *For you are sometimes darkness but now you are the light in the Lord, walk as the children of light. (Eph 5:8)*

> *Wherefore remember, that ye being in time past Gentiles in the flesh, who are called Uncircumcision by that which is called the Circumcision in the flesh made by hands; That at that time ye were without Christ, being aliens from the commonwealth of Israel, and strangers from the covenants of promise, having no hope, and without God in the world: But now in Christ Jesus ye who sometimes were far off are made nigh by the blood of Christ. (Eph 2:11-13)*

Life and Existence

Birth is good, but without life, it is sorrow. One birth that leads to life is better than several births that do not experience life. They merely exist, they do not live.

Those who do not know God's purpose for their lives merely exist. They do so well what they should not do at all, and they pursue everything except the reason for their life and living. God has made provision for every birth to lead to life and life to lead to abundant life. It does no good to experience one and not the other.

God wants us to prosper in body, soul, and spirit (3Jn 1:2). A life (physical or spiritual) that is weighed down with sickness or other burdens can be painful. But God has made adequate provision for this. It will be a shame to get to heaven to discover that half of what God has provided to be used on earth were returned unused or squandered. Jesus Himself went about doing good and healing all that were oppressed of the devil, for God was with Him (Act 10:38). He gave the disciples power to heal the sick and to deliver those who are oppressed of the devil (Mat 10:1, Mar 6:7,11, Luk 9:1). The provision is available for the church too:

> *Is any among you afflicted? let him pray. Is any merry? let him sing psalms. Is any sick among you? let him call for the elders of the church; and let them pray over him, anointing him with oil in the name of the Lord: And the prayer of faith shall save the sick, and the Lord shall raise him up; and if he have committed sins, they shall be forgiven him. (Jas 5:13-15)*

This is part of the abundant life for every believer. "No good thing will he withhold from them that walk uprightly." (Psa 84:11).

The disciples were confused about being a believer and being rich. At the end of Jesus' discourse with the rich young ruler, Jesus said it is easier for a camel to go through the eye of a needle than for a rich man to enter into the kingdom of God. (Mar 10:25) This confused the disciples about riches. In a confused state, Peter said, we have left all and follow you. But Jesus said:

> *There is no man that hath left house, or brethren, or sisters, or father, or mother, or wife, or children, or lands, for my sake, and the gospel's, But he shall receive an hundredfold now in this time, houses, and brethren, and sisters, and mothers, and children, and lands, with persecutions; and in the world to come eternal life. (Mar 10:29-30)*

God desires that we enter into the fullness of all His provisions for us, for His glory and for His name alone.

However, this does not mean that when we are in Christ, everything we want will be in place. I have heard people say that if you are sick or passing through challenging times, it's because God is not blessing you or your life is not pleasing to God. This is not true. Although God desires us to prosper and be in health as our soul prospers, but we cannot use transient things to judge eternal things. Paul said:

> *For we know that if our earthly house of this tabernacle were dissolved, we have a building of God, an house not made with hands, eternal in the heavens. For in this we groan, earnestly desiring to be clothed upon with our house which is from heaven: If so be that being clothed we shall not be found naked. For we that are in this tabernacle do groan, being burdened: not for that we would be unclothed, but clothed upon, that*

> *mortality might be swallowed up of life. Now he that hath wrought us for the selfsame thing is God, who also hath given unto us the earnest of the Spirit. Therefore we are always confident, knowing that, whilst we are at home in the body, we are absent from the Lord: (For we walk by faith, not by sight:) We are confident, I say, and willing rather to be absent from the body, and to be present with the Lord. Wherefore we labour, that, whether present or absent, we may be accepted of him. (2Cor 5:1-10)*

Anyone determined to go all out with God must be prepared to do it alone and unto death. This is the testimony of all the disciples. It does not mean that they were not approved of God. Even Jesus our master laid the example.

Many say that Jesus endured all that so that we will not have to experience it, but this is not consistent with the words of Jesus:

> *Think not that I am come to send peace on earth: I came not to send peace, but a sword. For I am come to set a man at variance against his father, and the daughter against her mother, and the daughter in law against her mother in law. And a man's foes shall be they of his own household. He that loveth father or mother more than me is not worthy of me: and he that loveth son or daughter more than me is not worthy of me. And he that taketh not his cross, and followeth after me, is not*

> *worthy of me. He that findeth his life shall lose it: and he that loseth his life for my sake shall find it. (Mat 10:34-39)*

When He died, we died with Him. We were in Him as He was crucified, nailed, beaten, buried, and we were raised from the dead with Him. We have His marks in our bodies, that is why although we are in the world, we are not of the world. We belonged to Him and we must not be conformed to this world.

> *Love not the world, neither the things that are in the world. If any man love the world, the love of the Father is not in him. For all that is in the world, the lust of the flesh, and the lust of the eyes, and the pride of life, is not of the Father, but is of the world. And the world passeth away, and the lust thereof: but he that doeth the will of God abideth for ever. (1Jo 2:15-17)*

God is sovereign in everything. We may not understand some things until by and by, but He is faithful, even when we are faithless and unfaithful and do not understand many things. Everything is for His glory (Joh 9:2).

Birth is the beginning of all things in the spirit. If there is no birth, there is no life. If there is truly life, there must be movement, there must be growth. Everything that has life grows. This is the beginning of a walk with God.

7

BASIC PRINCIPLES

"Therefore leaving the principles of the doctrine of Christ, let us go on unto perfection; not laying again the foundation of repentance from dead works, and of faith toward God, Of the doctrine of baptisms, and of laying on of hands, and of resurrection of the dead, and of eternal judgment."
- Hebrews 6:1-2

IN THE PREVIOUS chapters, we examined what the new birth is and what it is not. We laid the foundation of the true initiation into Christ's life, and that salvation cannot be conferred on anyone by any preacher, self or work. Salvation on its own is a free gift from God, and must be received by man in faith alone.

It is a false doctrine when we tell those who have just experienced the new birth that they are saved. How absurd this is in the light of the scriptures. It is more appropriate to say that they have begun the journey to salvation and they must keep on. The word "keep on" is key in the overall understanding of salvation; it is conditioned on "if" we keep on (Heb 3:6). When we infer that the new birth is salvation, it is like saying that when you obtain a letter of admission into a university, it is the same as the certificate of graduation. Once you have the letter, duly signed and stamped by the authority with your name and so on, you are already a graduate of that school and you can show everyone, use it to look for a job or hang it on the wall and call yourself a graduate of that school. You and I know that this is not how it works.

Confessing Christ as your Lord and personal Savior is the first step in the salvation or born again experience, but it is not the final. You have just obtained a provisional admission to the institution (of God). You have been called to learn, study, attend classes, write examinations and so on. Your graduation (salvation) is dependent on successful completion of these things, including passing the required examinations, which are the trials, tests, and tribulations of the saints. That is when you can say like Paul:

> *I have fought a good fight, I have finished my course, I have kept the faith: Henceforth there is laid up for me a crown of righteousness, which the Lord, the righteous judge, shall give me at that day: and not to me only, but unto all them also that love his appearing. (2Ti 4:7-8)*

This means that although salvation is free, you have a part to play by faith in order to keep it. Only then can you receive the crown.

To be saved is like to successfully complete the school requirement for graduation and be formally honored (crown of righteousness) as a graduate of the institution.

Believe

> *That if thou shalt confess with thy mouth the Lord Jesus, and shalt believe in thine heart that God hath raised him from the dead, thou shalt be saved. (Rom 10:9)*

The word "believe in your heart" conveys a much deeper spiritual reality than "confess with your mouth." That passage goes on to say:

> *For with the heart man believeth unto righteousness; and with the mouth confession is made unto salvation. (Rom 10:10)*

While anyone can confess anything with the mouth under any circumstance, without the belief in the heart, but to truly believe is to confess it with your mouth, even to death (1Ti 6:12).

It is what is believed in the heart that the mouth speaks. It becomes your profession. But when the word *believe* is not put in proper perspective, does not have the necessary spiritual depth, or is not conveyed with a sacrosanct divine understanding, it erodes the gravity and weightiness of it.

It can be misleading if to believe is presented as an intellectual accent (agreeing that certain facts are true) instead of as implicit trust (relying on those facts).

Judas Iscariot believed certain facts about Jesus, but he never trusted those facts enough to save him. In certain situations, he helped himself. John said: "he was a thief, and had the bag, and bare what was put therein." (Joh 12:6) Judas believed Jesus is the Messiah (Satan also believed that), but did not trust Him enough for his needs. So, in this context, even though Judas was a disciple of Jesus and followed Him for more than three years, he did not believe Jesus. This is a possibility for any believer.

Salvation is not about believing a list of facts about a savior. Making Jesus your Lord and personal Savior is a discovery of the fact that only Jesus can save you, but that requires a circumstantial and evidential working out. It is the working out that predicates the salvation, and it is an on-going exercise, proven at terrible times and situations, and yet not denying Him to the "day of the Lord."

Asking the Holy Spirit to come into your heart does not mean that you are saved. Many have done it several times and still doing it. Does it mean that they are being saved each time they do that?

The Holy Spirit will come into your heart if you ask Him to, but He comes to do certain things. What you allow Him to do in your life is what determines your salvation. One of His duties in your life is to show you the Father and lead you into all truths. Jesus said:

> *Howbeit when he, the Spirit of truth, is come, he will guide you into all truth: for he shall not speak of himself; but whatsoever he shall hear, that shall*

> *he speak: and he will shew you things to come. He shall glorify me: for he shall receive of mine, and shall shew it unto you. (Joh 16:13-14)*

Some people have the Holy Spirit for keep or as a testimony that they once had Him. Jesus can be in your boat but may be down in the basement, sleeping. He can be in your life and you are still in charge.

The disciples were on the sea when a great wind hit their boat. They were afraid and even despaired of life. They threw all their belongings, including food and so on into the sea, hoping that the water would assuage, but it did not. Finally, they lost hope. They then remembered that Jesus was in the boat:

> *He was in the hinder part of the ship, asleep on a pillow: and they awake him, and say unto him, Master, carest thou not that we perish? And he arose, and rebuked the wind, and said unto the sea, Peace, be still. And the wind ceased, and there was a great calm. And he said unto them, Why are ye so fearful? how is it that ye have no faith? And they feared exceedingly, and said one to another, What manner of man is this, that even the wind and the sea obey him? (Mar 4:38-41)*

Jesus was truly in their boat, but what they allowed Him to do circumstantially is the salvation they had. It is one thing to have Jesus as Savior, it is another to give Him the authority to lead you as Lord.

You may gain admission to a prestigious university but what determines if you are a graduate of that university is if you allow the university to make you into what it promised to. This is the same in the spirit: the Holy Spirit in you is to make you conform to the image and likeness of Christ, if you allow Him.

Salvation is not even about asking God to forgive you your sins. How many people have done that countless times and they still go back to the same life style. You probably have experienced that, too. He will surely forgive if you ask, but that does not mean you will not do it again. Salvation is a continuous thing: it is now, not something that happened to us sometimes ago or in view. The writer of the book of Hebrews sums it up like this:

> *But exhort one another daily, while it is called To day; lest any of you be hardened through the deceitfulness of sin. (Heb 3:13)*

The word "daily" and "today" are prominent. It goes further to say:

> *For we are made partakers of Christ, if we hold the beginning of our confidence stedfast unto the end. (Heb 3:14)*

As we have explained this verse in other chapter, it talks about two points: the beginning and the end. The connecting line between these points must be held stedfast to the end, and that is when salvation occurs. So every day, hour, moment counts.

So we see that salvation is now; it is today. The new birth can happen sometimes ago but salvation is always a current status, not a past experience. It is for those who keep on believing, till death, for those whose faith is based on what is happening or what will happen, not what happened (past). This does not mean that your keeping on believing or having faith that He will save you at the end is 'work,' it is depending on the Holy Spirit to do the 'work' in you. You must keep trusting Him to keep you going, otherwise, you can't make it on your own.

In Pawson's word:

> *Another pointer to the continuity of faith is to be found in the Greek tenses used for the verb 'believe'. When the initial step of faith that inaugurates the life of a believer is referred to, the aorist tense is used, referring to a single event or moment (examples may be found in Acts 16:31; 19:2). But on many occasions the present tense is used, indicating a continuous action or present, as distinct from a past condition. John is particularly fond of this second form: "For God so loved the world that he gave his one and only son, that whosoever believes [i.e. goes on believing, or is believing now] in him shall not perish but have [i.e. here and now, not just in the future – see v.36] eternal life' (John 3:16); 'The work of God is this: to believe [i.e. to go on believing, or to be believing] in the one he has sent' (John 6:29); 'But these are written that you may believe [i.e. go on*

> *believing or be believing] that Jesus is the Christ, the Son of God, and that by [going on] believing you may have [i.e. go on having] life in his name' (John 20:31). (Note that this makes John's gospel more suitable for believers than unbelievers, since its aim is to keep readers in faith rather than bring them to faith, which explains why it was written later than the three synoptics.)* [iv]

We must keep "looking unto Jesus the author and finisher of our faith." (Heb 12:1). Peter was able to walk on the water for as long as he was looking at Jesus. But when he took his eyes away from Him momentarily, he started to sink.

There are many things threatening to take our eyes away from Jesus. To Peter, it might be the wind, or just the sheer excitement that he was walking on water. These things will always be around us, and the more reason why we cannot afford to take our eyes away from Him for a moment. If we do, our faith (believing) will shipwreck (Mat 14:22-31, Heb 12:2).

The following scripture verses also buttress this truth.

> *Take heed, brethren, lest there be in any of you an evil heart of unbelief, in departing from the living God. But exhort one another daily, while it is called to day; lest any of you be hardened through the deceitfulness of sin. For we are made partakers of Christ, if we hold the beginning of our confidence stedfast unto the end; While it is said,*

> *To day if ye will hear his voice, harden not your hearts, as in the provocation. (Heb 1:12-15)*

The fire of yesterday is ashes of today. Therefore, to believe is an ongoing action that culminates at salvation. You cannot say: "I believed"; it has to be "I keep believing." It is a walk with Jesus that leads to glory, it is not a step to Jesus. This is just one and the same as sanctification: it is an ongoing process that culminates at holiness. Paul says:

> *Be ye transformed by the renewing of your mind. (Rom 12:2)*

Transformation (salvation) comes as your mind keeps renewing (sanctification).

Summarly, the first step in the renewing of your mind, which leads to holiness is to have a spiritual birth. This birth will lead you on the path of sanctification, which culminates at holiness. Thus, holiness is conferred by sanctification. Sanctification is not a one-time thing: it is an ongoing and never ending process until we meet our Lord and He pronounces us holy (Mat 5:48).

Chanting the sinners' prayer is just like a swearing or making a pledge or an oath of allegiance as a new student of the institution [of God]. It is a pledge to abide by the rules and to faithfully undertake the study. It must not be mistaken as being saved. This is the reason why the term *saved* has been grossly misused by those who just started this journey. You have just being initiated into the believing experience. Being born again is to make you a partaker of the very life (on going) of Christ, and again, "we are made partakers of Christ, if we hold the beginning of our confidence stedfast unto the end." (Heb 3:14) We must hold it to the end.

It is possible to believe the historical Jesus without having a spiritual and personal encounter with Him. When we present the facts about Jesus, His power and ability to save, deliver, war on our behalf, revoke curses, break covenants, prosper, heal, and at the end save us from hell and take us to heaven, and then ask if anyone would believe in Him. What do you expect? However, such a believe as this is hardly from the heart (Joh 6:26).

You can believe Him as a better and more powerful idol in order to use His name like medicine when in need. This does not mean that you love Him. You only love Him as long as He does what you expect. Believing is when He fails to do what you expect and you still believe Him (Job 13:15). It is not when you know who He is but when He also know who you are to Him. (Luk 13:27) Satan and his demons also believe Jesus, they even tremble.

A Process
At this juncture, let us look at the process of believing. According to the words of Jesus, "He that believeth and is baptized shall be saved, but he that believeth not shall be damned." (Mar 16:16) Paul, in Romans said that this believe must come from the heart. Yet the heart has become evil from the fall: "every imagination of the thoughts of his heart was only evil continually." (Gen 6:5) It has been reduced to a mere soul, devoid of the spirit, yet without the spirit, man

cannot know God, for "God is Spirit" and "it is the spirit that quickens."

When our heart is resolute and we keep believing, even though it takes passing through fire and Golgotha, that is when it really comes from the heart.

There are other ways many believe that is not from the heart. There is a traditional way: many would probably not be Christians today if they weren't born as Christians. That is why it is often possible that those who come to Christ from an entirely different religious persuasion may have actually had a genuine encounter with God if their coming is not the mere enticement of religion.

Many also must see before believing. This describes Thomas who insisted that except he saw Jesus and felt His scar with his fingers he would not believe that it was actually Him that rose from the dead. This type of belief is not blessed. Jesus said to Thomas:

> *Because thou hast seen me, thou hast believed: blessed are they that have not seen, and yet have believed. (Joh 20:29)*

Some others believe Jesus so that He can satisfy their needs. If He no longer does, they will look for someone else who can.

King Nebuchadnezzar compelled everyone to either bow to his image or be thrown into the burning furnace:

> *Shadrach, Meshach, and Abednego, answered and said to the king, "O Nebuchadnezzar, we are not careful to answer thee in this matter. If it be*

> *so, our God whom we serve is able to deliver us from the burning fiery furnace, and he will deliver us out of thine hand, O king. But if not, be it known unto thee, O king, that we will not serve thy gods, nor worship the golden image which thou hast set up. (Dan 3:16-18)*

So we see what to believe from the heart really is. But it is impossible to just believe without first having an encounter with God.

Encounter with God
When Adam sinned in the Garden of Eden, he was estranged from God. He could no longer hear the voice of God, have fellowship or commune with Him in the cool of the day as he used to. But despite this alienation, it was amazing that Adam still heard God when God called him to know where he was.

God called out to Adam as if He did not know where he was or what had happened to him and Eve. Although man died a spiritual death, God was still gracious and merciful to him; He still left a part of Himself in man, a thin connection where He could give him the 'last call,' as it were. He would not entirely abandon him, otherwise, man would be entirely lost.

The divine part of God is in every man. It is what Father God uses to draw people to Himself. This is what Jesus means when He says no man can come to Him except His Father draws him. (Joh 6:44) The spark is the "draw' and it is only the Father that draws people to Jesus, not the preachers. Preachers cannot even bring themselves to Christ, let alone bring others to Him. The Greek word for draw is *helkuo helko* and it literally mean "to drag." Jesus said:

> *And this is the Father's will which hath sent me, that of all which he hath given me I should lose nothing, but should raise it up again at the last day. (Joh 6:39)*

For this reason, our message to people must be to challenge them to stand to face God. It is then that sinners realize how lost they are and that they are on the highway to the lake of fire, and also that God has made a way for them to return to Him and that way is Christ (not Christianity). The spark will ignite a longing for the Father in their hearts, and also make them to see the gulf between them and the loving Father: they cannot just return by themselves, they need a savior to bring them across the gulf, to escape the lake of fire and bring them to the Father.

God lovingly waits with outstretched arms at the other side, desiring to see the lost come back to Him. He points them to the Savior who would bring them to Him. Everyone that comes to God is through this process. This is the genuine way of coming to Christ, it has to be through God. Then, God leads you to His Son, Jesus, the only Way He has provided for mankind to come to Him. Just as the passage we have quoted before:

> *No man can come to me, except the Father which hath sent me draw him. (Joh 6:44)*

> *... My Father, which gave them me, is greater than all; and no man is able to pluck them out of my Father's hand. (Joh 10:29)*

It means that if we do not stand to face God, and in trusting faith allow His light to shine for us to see the path He has made for us to come to Him, we cannot really see or know who Jesus is. Paul said:

> *For it is God which worketh in you both to will and to do of his good pleasure. (Php 2:13)*

Only the *spark* (power) of God can bring sinners to his knees and weep before God saying:

> *Woe is me! for I am undone; because I am a man of unclean lips, and I dwell in the midst of a people of unclean lips: for mine eyes have seen the King, the LORD of hosts. (Isa 6:5)*

This is where we see ourselves as the filthy rags that we indeed are, and then the need for help arises. That is when God can reach out to us.

> *For the preaching of the cross is to them that perish foolishness; but unto us which are saved it is the power of God. (1Co 1:18)*

Below is the highlight of what having an encounter with God does in a believer's life. They are the seven fundamental truths of salvation.

Man must realize that:

1. He is lost. This is not because of the sinful choices he makes but because he was born lost. When a man realizes this, he just had an encounter with God.
2. He needs to return home to the Father. God is our Father and desires all men to return to Him. This reality is repentance sparked by godly sorrow.
3. He cannot return by himself because there is a gulf that separates him and God.
4. He needs someone (a savior) to take him through the gulf (lake of fire) and bring him to God successfully. Many lords and religions occupy and claim this position in deceit.
5. God causes His light to shine on the lost sinner and he discovers that only Jesus Christ can do it, no one else. This is because God sent only Jesus for that specific assignment.
6. He discovers that Jesus is qualified to do it because He paid the price with His blood and possess the right equipment (the cross) to take him across and to God.
7. All he needs do is to trust and follow Him without a doubt. He will take him to God based on what He (Jesus) did and not on what he (man) did, doing and will do.

Saul, who later became Paul was busy pursuing 'dead works;' he was doing God a 'service' without His will when he had his own encounter.

> *And Saul, yet breathing out threatenings and slaughter against the disciples of the Lord, went unto the high priest, And desired of him letters to Damascus to the synagogues, that if he found any of this way, whether they were men or women, he might bring them bound unto Jerusalem. (Act 9:1-2)*

There and then, Saul discovered how wrong and how lost he was, and he cried out for help, saying: "Lord, what do you want me to do?" (Act 9:6). When he rose, he was a completely different person: he had met God. All the supposed noble works, efforts, and services he was doing for God was indeed a curse to him and he was truly like filthy rags.

But notice that in that encounter, Saul called Him "Lord" even though he never met Him. Anyone who truly have this encounter will recognize Jesus as Lord. This is because it is an innate working of the Spirit in the heart. You will know that truly, you have met the Lord.

Let me ask you this question: how did you come to Christ? Did you pass through these seven fundamental truths or just some? Did you come through church or denominational attraction? Did you come through the appeal of program? Is it because of personal problems or trouble? Is it a need for healing, deliverance or breakthrough that brought you to Him?

If your answer is not because you have an encounter with God through these fundamental truths, you might want to consider your salvation in good faith. It is better to be sure now than to be sorry in eternity. It will be too late to discover this in heaven. Encounter leads to repentance, if you did not have this encounter, you cannot have godly sorrow that leads to repentance. (2Co 7:10)

If you ever met Him, you will fear Him, for you know that "it is a fearful thing to fall into the hands of the living God." (Heb 10:31) His fear will prevent you from sin. You will say like Joseph: "how then can I do this great wickedness, and sin against God?" (Gen 39:9) You will realize that all sins are ultimately against God. His love will melt your heart and you will seek to love Him and never want to hurt Him. This love will break the power of sin or besetting sins in your life forever.

Repentance from dead works

> *Therefore leaving the principles of the doctrine of Christ, let us go on unto perfection; not laying again the foundation of repentance from dead works, and of faith toward God, of the doctrine of baptisms, and of laying on of hands, and of resurrection of the dead, and of eternal judgment. (Heb 6:1-2)*

In this passage, the writer of the book of Hebrews was obviously writing to believers. He expected them to already know what he was saying as regards the "principles of the doctrines of Christ," so he charged them to leave that, and He said to them: "let us go on unto perfection." Even though he declared that there was no need to lay the foundation of the principles of the doctrine of Christ again, he still went on to highlight what these principles are in sequential order. First, repentance from dead works…

Repentance from dead works occurs when you have an encounter with God. I so much appreciate the way David Pawson puts it and the particular word used to describe it. He sums it up this way:

> *The word "repent" (Greek: metanoeo) means literally to change one's mind. It means to think again, particularly with reference to past behavior.*
>
> *… To repent means to think about things from God's point of view, to agree with his analysis and accept his verdict. It is to say 'Yes' to God's 'Yes', and assent to His 'No'. It is to learn to say 'Amen' to God's word. It is to have a clear vision of human sin, measured by the standard of divine righteousness and the inevitable judgment that must take place when the two meet (John 16:8). It is to come to a 'knowledge of the truth' (2Tim 2:25) about God and about one's self.* [v]

I like to say that repentance is when you see God as who He really is and also see yourself as who you really are. But sadly today, the message of repentance has been de-emphasized in the preaching of the Gospel. People are not being challenged to face God. Consequently, many *believers* never really know God. This perhaps explains why there is so much Christianity in people but less godliness. Repentance is mostly preached in relation to believers confessing their wrongs or sins. But the real meaning of repentance suggests that it is for unbeliever to turn to God, away from primordial perdition and from death unto life.

To truly believe Christ from your heart means that at one time or the other, you had an encounter with God, for only God touches the heart. This leads to godly sorrow and then repentance.

The part I like most in Pawson's explanation of repentance is this:

> *At one level, this discovery will be in general terms. On the one hand, a person will become deeply aware that God is much better than he is generally thought to be. The Lord is absolutely holy, absolutely pure, absolutely just. On the other hand, a person will become painfully aware that he himself is much, much worse than he thought he was. Instead of thinking of himself as basically a good person who has done bad things from time to time, (the 'humanist' view), he discovers he is basically a bad person who has managed to do some good things from time to time (Jesus' view of human nature – Luke 11:13; cf John 2:24). Worse than that, even the good things he has done can be as offensive to God as the bad and need also to be repented of (Isa 64:6 describes human righteousness as a menstrual cloth; Phil 3:8 describes it in terms of human excreta!) This discovery, that God finds self-righteousness more offensive and intractable than crude sin comes*

> *as a great shock to human pride and completes the revolution in thought inherent in true repentance.* [vi]

As we can see, repentance means to see yourself exactly how God sees you. It is broader than repenting from the sin of lying, stealing or even much less or greater sins. It is seeing yourself that you cannot but sin. It is seeing the good that you do is more offensive to God. It is a discovery of who God is: a twice holy God and that you are a born sinner, not because of the sin you commit, but you commit sin because you are a sinner. And you need God to help you, and if He does not, you are doomed.

The greatest sin is the sin of self, me, mine and I. It is when we are full of self that we take our eyes away from God, because without Him, we can do nothing. This is the beginning of the downfall of Satan and also of Adam and Eve in the Garden. Consequently, this is the first sin we have to repent of without which we cannot even come to God. It is the pride of man, which magnifies what he can do.

When we repent of the like sins of murder, genocide, abortion, and so on, without having first repented of the first, which is the *original sin*, we cannot receive forgiveness. This is so because sinners cannot even stand before God to confess their sins. God does not hear sinners (Joh 9:31), that is, those who have not yet repented of the *original* sin.

It is pride to think that we can return home to God from our lost state without Him. It's a commendable try, but spiritual things are not trial and error; that is religion. It is pride to think that we can break the power of sin by ourselves without

His power. Such people will keep on committing sins because they are still under the curse of the first sin, which can only be broken when we turn 180 degrees to God. It is after man is cleared of the first sin, as it were, and he is in right standing with God, that he can stand to ask for forgiveness of all other sins that he commits subsequently, and can receive forgiveness. But as long as one is yet to repent of the first sin, he is a sinner, even though he does not commit those things we know as sin like murder, fornication, etc.

So every man must first turn to God: from going South to heading North, from death to life, from Satan to God. You must be in the camp of God first before you talk to Him about your sins and besetting sins. But if you are still in the original sin, even if you repent with sacrifices and burnt offering of a genuine heart, God cannot hear you because you are taking the cart before the horse. God calls the "genuine heart": "deceitful above all things and desperately wicked: who can know it." You are in the opposite direction with God and He cannot hear you. You are still a sinner and the eyes of sinners will not see the glory of God. But having repented of the original sin and you already turned to God, if you sin, you can confess your sins, repent and be forgiven. John wrote thus:

> *My little children, these things write I unto you, that ye sin not. And if any man sin, we have an advocate with the Father, Jesus Christ the righteous. (1Jo 2:1)*

The sin John is talking about here is believers who fall into wrong-doing or miss the mark after the new birth. What we need to do is to confess the sin because we already have access to Him, even though we fall, we can receive forgiveness and rise again.

Dead works, however refer to your good morals, your effort in trying to please God by observing certain things and your religious works. It is all religion to God. Religion is the way man has devised to get to God. It is the opposite of faith, which God has devised for man to get to Him.

Religion and good works are dead because they cannot save, even though they are good. Salvation is "not of works, lest any man should boast." (Eph 2:9) When you see God the way He really is and you see yourself who you really are, you will come to the place of saying:

> *Woe is me! for I am undone; because I am a man of unclean lips, and I dwell in the midst of a people of unclean lips: for mine eyes have seen the King, the LORD of hosts. (Isa 6:5).*
>
> *You will come to the understanding that the best work you have is truly like a menstrual cloth or human excreta to God. (Isa 64:6, Phil 3:8)*

Godly sorrow WORKS repentance, but it is not repentance by itself, and repentance on its own is not salvation. (2Co 7:10)

The early church understood that to believe in the heart is a process that involves repentance from dead works. John the

Baptist preached it (Joh 3:2). Jesus preached it (Mat 4:7). Paul preached it (Act 20:21, 2Co 7:9-10). Peter preached it (Act 2:38, 2Pe 3:9). The disciples preached it (Mar 6:12). The early church preached it, but the end time church is missing it. We bring people to Jesus by-passing God, yet everything begins with God. It is God that brings us to Himself through Christ. Without Him calling us, we cannot come to Him on our own (Joh 6:65). Since man is lost by default and cannot return home to God by Himself, the benevolence and mercies of God has made a way for man to return to Him. This is at a great cost to Him but no cost to us other than to accept it by faith as a free gift.

Godliness
Many claim to have received Jesus as Lord and Savior, but their lives and character do not show that they even know God. They speak the Christian slang, language, do all the Christian works and are even zealous in church and activities. Some may even be leaders, but somehow, you cannot reconcile their lives with godliness.

Let us look at Nigeria as a case study. According to a survey in a particular year, Nigeria was adjudged to be the 'most religious country in the world.' I do not know what measures were used to determine this but looking *inside* the country, there seems to be more pastors than the congregation, more church meetings than secular meetings. In many cities, there are several churches in almost every street. There are instances of several different denominational churches renting different floors of the same building, each trying to outdo the other, devising and organizing ingenious programs to woo *customers and investors.*

In the same vein, at one time, Nigeria was reputed to have the largest Christian gathering on earth and also has the largest Christian auditorium. Lately, she is said to have the richest pastor on earth. There is much [unbelievable] opulence with many of the leaders who pastor hundreds of thousands of those hoping to be blessed by God, just as the pastor is, but at the cost of the little they have, which they must give to the pastor in order to be blessed.

The irony of all these is that the same nation is said to be one of the most corrupt nations on earth, and sadly, it can be seen from the church. Many of the churches have empires that the members of the congregation can only get to in their dream and imagination. They have institutions that members cannot attend because of cost. Most of these pastors cannot be accessed because they have become more or less a god. Consequently, there is no discernable difference between the church and the society. There seemed to be more righteousness in the society before the advent of the proliferation of churches than now. The shocking ungodliness perpetuated by many of these leaders makes one to raise queries and doubt the charade.

This is not peculiar to this nation. The comfort is that there are many who love the Lord in spirit, in truth, and in sincerity in all the places these happen. They are sick and tired of the whole show as it was with Lot in Sodom. They are the remnant.

In another extreme case, recent statistics showed that Nigeria has the highest religion-related deaths in the world in the last few years. This is mainly due to the activities of *Boko Haram*, an Islamic fundamentalist sect whose name literally means "western education is forbidden." They derive joy in killing, maiming and dismembering people, especially Christians. In 2014, they abducted more than 200 high school Christian girls and they are yet to be seen as at the time of writing this book. It has been speculated that they used them as suicide bombers, human shields in combat or marry them off to their members so as to give birth to children who are radicalized from birth. The majority of these girls are in their early teens. The main agenda of the sect is to Islamize the country and enforce the Sharia penal code. They are said to be the most deadly terrorist group in the world, more deadly than ISIS.

While there seems to be no answer to all these barbaric incidences, Paul was of the same mindset before he came to Christ. He was also consumed by the zeal of religion. He wanted to make everyone a Judaizer, just like the Muslim extremists would make everyone a Muslim. According to their religion, anyone who is not a Muslim must be killed and there is a reward for killing such "infidels."

It was said that young Muslims are radicalized by outrageous religious enticements. An example is that those who die as martyrs for the cause of Islam will be rewarded with 72 virgins in paradise! Perhaps this explains the reasons why many accept to be suicide bombers. It is a cheap way to have what they always lusted after on earth but could not get. Would having such sensual pleasure in heaven be enough reason to lose one's life on earth! The Bible says: "For in the resurrection they neither marry, nor are given in marriage, but are as the angels of God in heaven." (Mat 22:30)

Saul also "made havoc of the church, entering into every house, and hauling men and women committed them to prison." (Act 8:3). He was moved by similar extreme religious zeal. All zeal does is to destroy. (Psa 69:9, Psa 119:139, Rom 10:2, 2Co 3:6)

This is the characteristic of practicing a religion without an encounter with God. Until Paul had an encounter, he thought he was doing God a service. It means that God can still save members of these Islamic groups scattered around the world carrying out many of these dastardly activities in the name of religion.

Many who claim to be Christians and are yet ungodly have perhaps not met Christ or they came in through the back door. Either way, their Christian cycle will be abnormal in nature. Some might probably have a genuine birth that did not lead to life. This may be due to various reasons including unskilled (spiritual) midwifery.

Many untrained personnel midwife births in a quack and criminal way that exposes the newly born to untold hardship in life, if he ever survived. Babies from such deliveries become (spiritually) disabled, needing assisted living for life. Many have been infected with deadly (spiritual) virus during delivery. Unfortunately, there are many centers opened by such quack midwives (pastors). They take delivery from inexperienced mothers (members) sometimes for the sole purpose of counting how many births they have, not minding how many truly survived. It is a case of many births, but few lives. Where there is no life, there cannot be abundant life.

The first step in the process of believing in God is thus repentance from dead works. Only when this happens can anything that has to do with God be possible. This leads to the next step in the process of believing: faith towards God.

Faith towards God
According to the order in Hebrews 6, after repentance from dead works, following it is faith towards God. This is not just a mere coincidence, it is actually the next thing.

Man has repented of the original sin. He has turned 180 degrees, from death to life. He now desires to return home to God, but there is a great gulf separating him and God. At this junction of decision, he stands before God in absolute faith and surrender, hoping, praying and trusting God to come take him across the bridge to Himself. This is where the need for a savior arises. Unfortunately, there are many 'saviors,' many ways and many doors, waiting and beckoning (Pro 14:12) This is where faith is required: to stand in faith and trust that God will lead you to the right Savior. Only Jesus Christ is The Way, The Door, The Truth and the Life (Joh 14:6).

Any decision or choice man makes on his own at this point is a wrong one. This is because man is incapable of choosing right or choosing God by default since the fall.

Paul, writing to the Philippian Church, warned them to be careful of "another Jesus," "another Gospel," and "another spirit." (2Co 11:4) These truly exist. Jesus also warned that many would rise and claim that they are Christ and if it were possible would deceive the very elect (Mar 13:6, 21, Mat 24:24). This is the junction where all religions of the world beckons, attracting innocent souls with their glory and allure. The New Age religion and other pseudo-religions also stand, parading their piety, righteousness and salvation. But none of these save, including Christian religion. Religion does not save. Systems do not save. Only a Person saves, and that is Jesus! He says:

> *I am the way, the truth, and the life: no man cometh unto the Father, but by me. (Joh 14:6)*

Paul warned:

> *That your faith should not stand in the wisdom of men, but in the power of God. (1Co 2:5)*

Any chance to choose through the human faculty, reasoning, logic or wisdom will lead one astray; it will lead to death and destruction. The gods of this world are standing to prevent the light of the glorious gospel from shining to many at this point.

> *The god of this world hath blinded the minds of them which believe not, lest the light of the glorious gospel of Christ, who is the image of God, should shine unto them. (2Co 4:4)*

They manifest as angel of light and present their own light of religion to helpless souls.

> *And no marvel; for Satan himself is transformed into an angel of light. Therefore it is no great thing if his ministers also be transformed as the ministers of righteousness; whose end shall be according to their works. (2Co 11:14-15)*

Many miss it at this junction. You must stand in faith towards God, and say like Moses: "we will not leave this place unless your presence goes with us."

For anyone who stands in faith towards God, God sees the faith and He is pleased because "without faith it is impossible to please God." (Heb 11:6) He causes the light of the glorious gospel to shine on Jesus. The light does not shine on any religion, not even on Christianity. Because the light is from God, it can only lead to His Son, Jesus. That is who God gave (Joh 3:16) It also brings inner conviction and joy as evidence. This conviction makes you to put your whole trust in Him alone, knowing that there is no other person, way, door or savior. It is a defiant faith, a reckless faith, a faith that trusts totally, abandoning one's life and eternity to Him, because you see through God's eyes. You see where all other ways and doors lead to. You have had an encounter with Jesus. You know Him. You saw Him. You met Him and that is your faith, your trust and your testimony.

Harvesters

God asks us to pray to Him so He may send laborers to harvest, not to plant souls (Mat 9:38). He does the planting by

Himself (1Co 3:11). He only calls us to reap where we have not sown (Joh 4:38). God did not ask us to go save people but to tell them about His saving power, and He will save them.

The souls belong to God: He knows what to do with them. If we will stop trying to save people with our programs, messages, and so on, God will be able to save as many as He wills. Teachers and Preachers must realize that they are not the Savior. Although they have passion and zeal for God and desire to bring soul to the kingdom, the zeal must be with knowledge, to do exactly as instructed, not to formulate or device own methods of helping to bring souls to the kingdom. We should present the gospel and allow God to do the rest. Can we even save ourselves? How come we are trying to save others!

However, this is not a license to a passive resolve to abandon what is generally regarded as 'The Great Commission.' If we do not go out to tell people about the plan of God and His provision to save through Jesus, how will people have encounter with God and how will God save them to Himself through His Son. How will they hear if we do not go?

Salvation
In summary, we have examined one of the two basic principles and requirements of salvation: to believe. It is a process that begins with an encounter with God through the spark of God in every man. The encounter makes us to see who God really is and who we really are; that we are lost. This leads to godly sorrow that brings repentance (from dead works). We no longer trust in our own efforts to return to

God. We no longer trust that our morals and 'good works,' can save us. We now stand and wait on God to lead us through the way He has provided for the lost son to come back home to Him. This standing and waiting is Faith towards God: to lead us to the right savior.

The other requirement of salvation is to 'be baptized.' We will treat this in the subsequent chapter. It is until these two processes are experienced that salvation is in view, according to Mark 16:16.

Although many do not subscribe to the doctrine of the eternal security of the believer, but to think that coming to Christ or experiencing birth in the born again process is salvation is even worse. The basic principles of the doctrines of Christ as contained in Hebrews chapter six puts the very first step in the doctrines of salvation as to believe, and then to be baptized. These processes are one after the other. We cannot proceed to the next until we have fully experienced the previous. Many times, God does not show the next step until we take the previous step. Faith is climbing the steps even when you do not see the stairs.

> *For the preaching of the cross is to them that perish foolishness; but unto us which are saved it is the power of God. (1Co 1:18)*

8

THE SPIRIT REALITY

*"Except a man be born of water and of the Spirit,
he cannot enter into the kingdom of God."*
- **John 3:5**

Baptisms

IN THE PREVIOUS chapter, we examined the first requirement for salvation, to believe. In this chapter, we will examine the second requirement, to be baptized.

Baptism is the second requirement for salvation and the third in the basic principles of the doctrines of Christ. It is called "the doctrine of baptisms." (Heb 6:2) Notice that it is plural. Jesus also confirmed this when He told Nicodemus:

> *Except a man be born of water and of the Spirit, he cannot enter into the kingdom of God. (Joh 3:5)*

There are two types of baptisms: water and spirit.

Water Baptism

Many people think that water baptism is just a ritual, a type and shadow of *real* baptism, which is the spirit baptism. But consistently in the scriptures, especially in the book of the Acts of the Apostles, we see that new believers were baptized in water (Acts 2:41, 8:12, 13,16, 36, 38, Acts 9:18, Acts 10:47, 48, Acts 11:16, Acts 16:15, 33, Acts 18:8, Acts 19:3,4, 5, Acts 22:16).

Since the early church practiced it, there is no reason why we should not embrace it. A believer that is not water baptized is like an un-interned corpse. Imagine living with a corpse that is not or not properly buried. The stench can only be imagined. If we are dead in Christ, it is proper for us to be buried in Him. I believe that many believers may not be able to display the aroma and the fragrance of Christ without water baptism because they will have struggles in the flesh. They will battle with besetting sins and this will hinder them to live a life of victory in Christ. According to Bern Zumpano:

> *The word "baptize" comes from the Greek New Testament word "baptizo", which means "to be overwhelmed by." Sinking ships and people alike, when they go down under the water, are "overwhelmed" by the water. The water totally and completely engulfs their very being of what they are.* [vii]

Water baptism fulfills the righteousness of God in a believer. He identifies with Christ in His death when he enters into the water, and when he rises, he identifies with His resurrection. Our old-self with its sin nature is buried (Rom 5:3-4), and our new man is resurrected. We rise into the life of Christ, no longer our own lives. (Gal 3:27)

It does no good if we go into the water and do not experience the power of the Spirit. Water baptism has its own benefits, which more or less is an outward declaration of the inward manifestation. There is no reason why a believer would deliberately not want to be water baptized if there is an opportunity and no known hindrance.

Many people refer to the thief on the right side of Jesus who did not have the opportunity to be baptized, yet Jesus said to him:

> *Verily I say unto thee, Today shalt thou be with me in paradise. (Luk 23:43)*

Although this case has been explained in earlier chapter, but it is not too much to add that aside from the fact that this was a special case, this man did not belong to the dispensation of the church, he was of the dispensation of Israel, so he did not need baptism to be saved. All anyone needed to do to make "paradise" then was to either fulfill the law or believe Jesus.

> *But to him that worketh not, but believeth on him that justifieth the ungodly, his faith is counted for righteousness. (Rom 4:5)*

This man had no "good work" and he was actually a breaker of the law, but he believed "on him that justifieth the ungodly." So, he became righteous. This man was not part of the church and yet had assurance of heaven. Salvation then, was to keep the law or believe Jesus, even as Abraham believed God, and it was accounted to him for righteousness (Gal 3:6, Rom 4:3, Jas 2:23). He should, therefore, not be used as an excuse or example of anyone who did not have water baptism because the church would not begin until Pentecost.

John the Baptist's major work was to introduce Jesus and the new dispensation. He baptized people to foreshadow something to come, which had no comparison. He could only allude the overwhelming experience of what he saw but indescribable to a total emersion and hence, to dunk people in water was the closest physical expression to what is coming. He said:

> *I indeed baptize you with water unto repentance. But he that cometh after me is mightier than I, whose shoes I am not worthy to bear: he shall baptize you with the Holy Ghost, and with fire. (Mat 3:11)*

John's baptism was for Repentance for the sins of the people. But they still required works to fulfill and maintain the law:

> *Bring forth therefore fruits meet for repentance: And think not to say within yourselves, We have Abraham to our father: for I say unto you, that God is able of these stones to raise up children unto Abraham. And now also the axe is laid unto the root of the trees: therefore every tree which bringeth not forth good fruit is hewn down, and cast into the fire. (Mat 3:8-10)*

However, the baptism of Jesus is by trusting faith: identifying with His death, burial and resurrection, and also receiving

His spirit in order to walk in power. This means that before you get to the stage of baptism, which is the third in the list of the basic doctrines of Christ, (foundation of repentance from dead works, faith toward God and the doctrine of baptisms which we are treating now), you must have passed through the first and the second (repentance from dead works and faith towards).

The baptism-in-the-Holy Spirit is a separate and distinct experience from the new birth (repentance and faith). It represents the Holy Spirit's empowerment to walk the spiritual faith walk in the power of the Spirit Himself. It represents the re-establishment of the spiritual communication with the Spirit of God, which was broken off in Adam and Eve in the Garden of Eden through the Fall.

When Jesus told Nicodemus that "Except a man be born of water and of the Spirit, he cannot enter into the kingdom of God," (Joh 3:5) He was pointing him to an experience of a latter reality. Nicodemus did not understand it and would not. He could understand being born of water. He probably had seen or heard of John the Baptist before and many going to him to be baptized by him in Judea. But he would never understand being born of the Spirit.

> *Nicodemus saith unto him, how can a man be born when he is old? Can he enter the second time into his mother's womb, and be born? (Joh 3:4)*

One major reason why the understanding of this man, and indeed everyone then, was limited is that "the Spirit" had not yet been given. The Spirit baptism is specifically for the church, not for Israel. Besides, Jesus was still alive with the ministry to the Jews, Pentecost was still in view.

John shed a little bit of light on this in a separate event of Jesus:

> *He that believeth on me, as the scripture hath said, out of his belly shall flow rivers of living water. (But this spake he of the Spirit, which they that believe on him should receive: for the Holy Ghost was not yet given; because that Jesus was not yet glorified. (Joh 7:38-39)*

He that believes Jesus will have a spiritual reality he described as "living water," not just ordinary water from outside but from within (out of his belly), not from Judea. The baptism of John was an outward working and evidence but the Holy Spirit's working is from in to out.

It follows that even if Nicodemus was baptized in water, he could still not be baptized in the Spirit. John confessed that the spirit baptism was a future event and he himself could not do it. (Mat 3:11)

None of the disciples were baptized in the spirit nor could be, as long as Jesus was with them. It was only possible if He left. He said to them:

> *I will pray the Father, and he shall give you another Comforter, that he may abide with you for ever; But the Comforter, which is the Holy Ghost, whom the Father will send in my name, he shall teach you all things, and bring all things to*

your remembrance, whatsoever I have said unto you... Nevertheless I tell you the truth; It is expedient for you that I go away: for if I go not away, the Comforter will not come unto you; but if I depart, I will send him unto you. (Joh 14:16, Joh 14:26, Joh 16:7)

Jesus charged the disciples:

Tarry ye in the city of Jerusalem, until ye be endued with power from on high. (Luk 24:49)

And when the day of Pentecost was fully come, they were all with one accord in one place. And suddenly there came a sound from heaven as of a rushing mighty wind, and it filled all the house where they were sitting. And there appeared unto them cloven tongues like as of fire, and it sat upon each of them. And they were all filled with the Holy Ghost, and began to speak with other tongues, as the Spirit gave them utterance. (Act 2:1-4)

The Manifestation
The message of Jesus to Nicodemus to be born of the spirit then leaves us with much comprehension. We must see how and where the reality of it is applicable. The short summary of it is that its manifestation could only be in the church. At the time Jesus told Nicodemus this, the church was not yet birthed. Only the church has the promise of the spirit and that means only the church can have the experience of being born of the spirit.

To have a clearer understanding of this, we must go back to the early church to know how this promise came to reality and manifestation in their time, and how they were actually baptized in the Spirit.

One major factor that makes this possible for them was that Jesus had left at this time and fulfilled His promise to send the Spirit. The Holy Spirit was around and active. He was no longer a future reality to them but a present manifestation. And He will be active till the Rapture of the church. He is the seal and the quickening Spirit that will make believers to be caught up to meet the Lord in the air (Eph 4:30, Rom 8:11, 1Th 4:17).

In examining the book of the Gospels, we see that they point to a coming reality of the life of Christ through His Spirit to come. We may therefore not find the direct fulfillment or manifestation of the Spirit in the Gospels. This is because the Holy Spirit only embodied Jesus for miracles, healings and so on at the time of the Gospels. (Act 10:38)

If we consider the Epistles, we only see references and allusions to the experience and manifestations of the Spirit in the church. It shows us that the church manifested in the Spirit but did not tell us how they did it or experienced it. This is because the epistles were written to the already established churches, those who had at one time or the other experienced the Spirit and were already living the life of Christ as the church.

Again, going back to our text in Hebrews, the writer highlighted an assumption of knowledge of the basic principles of the doctrine of Christ, which were the foundation for believers (Heb 6:1-2). The charge was for believers: those who already had the experience of the Spirit and were already living the life of Christ. It was assumed that they already knew the principles and there was no need to go over it again, only just for a mention. It was assumed that they not only had the birth experience but the life experience. He was therefore challenging them for more: the abundant life. He said to them: "Let us go on unto perfection; not laying again the foundation…"

The foundations had been laid. Birth had occurred. People were already in the church, functioning, growing and experiencing the life of Christ. But there was need for maturity, abundant life, which is the door to eternal life. This is what they were being challenged into.

However, the challenge for perfection may not be relevant to the church today. While he says, *"not laying again the foundation…"* the truth is that the reverse is the case with the end time church. We have to lay the foundation again and again. And we cannot proceed to perfection yet until that is well laid.

The greatest challenge of the end time church is that the foundation and the basic principles are no longer taught or taught wrongly. An example is the born again experience which we have tried to set straight in the course of this book. How can we move on to abundant life, maturity or perfection when the foundation for the basic principles is not in place?

This follows that we really cannot know how the Spirit baptism was experienced in the Gospels because it was too early and pointing to the coming manifestation of the Spirit. Similarly, we cannot know it in the Epistles because it was too late: the letters were written to the already established churches: to encourage them to go on with the life of Christ they already had. The book of Revelation points to basically post-church events, so it cannot be really considered for this.

Again, quoting Pawson, he puts it this way:

> *Surprisingly, the events related in the gospels are too early for our purpose. Covering the period between the advent and ascension of Jesus. The gospels cannot give us a full picture of the normal pattern of initiation as understood by the post-Pentecostal church (which is the precedent for the "age" in which we also live)*
>
> *...but the epistles and Revelation are too late for our purpose. All of these writings were addressed to believers who had already been initiated*
>
> *A good starting-point*
>
> *So, if the gospels are too early and the epistles too late for our staring point, what are we left with? The book of Acts! It is the only book in the New Testament to major on post-Pentecostal evangelism. It is full of detail about how unbelievers became believers, how sinners became saints. It is the record of the divine and human aspect of salvation, telling us about the acts of the Apostles*

in bringing Christ to people and the acts of the Spirit in bringing people to Christ. [viii]

Fulfilled at Pentecost

However, looking into the book of the Acts of the Apostles, which is actually the acts of the church, we will not only see how the Spirit came, but also how people received the Spirit baptism which is part of how to be born again. So, the book of Acts of the Apostles give the vivid, live and on-site manifestation and present experience of believers and the early church in receiving the baptism of the Holy Spirit (Act 1:5, 2:38, 19:3-5, 8:13, 8:36, 9:18, 10:47, 16:15, 16:33, 18:8).

We see that the message of Jesus to Nicodemus was a future reality, which began to manifest in the Acts of the church when the Holy Spirit took over. It began at Pentecost with the disciples and then to the church and then to us at the last days.

But why would Jesus ask Nicodemus to do what he could not do in his dispensation? It is no different a reason than why He asked the rich young ruler to go sell all he had, give to the poor and follow Him. Jesus did not tell the young ruler to be born of water and spirit like he told Nicodemus. He only told him that he needed to be in the dispensation of grace in order to "be perfect." Earlier, He had told him what he needed to do to "enter eternal life." It was the dispensation of the law and all he or anyone needed to do to inherit eternal life at this dispensation was to keep the law. Jesus told him:

> *Thou knowest the commandments, do not commit adultery, Do not kill, Do not steal, Do not*

> *bear false witness, Defraud not, Honor thy father and mother. (Mar 10:19)*

Although, it was impossible to keep the law and no man could keep it, not even the Pharisees who prided themselves in keeping the law, but this man claimed he had kept all the laws from his youth!

> *Then Jesus beholding him loved him. (Mar 10:21)*

This statement did not occur often in the Bible where Jesus loved a religious person as a result of his religious activity. The love must have moved Him to introduce this man to grace: a new dispensation beyond the man's generation. He told him:

> *If thou wilt be perfect, go and sell that thou hast, and give to the poor, and thou shalt have treasure in heaven: and come and follow me. (Mat 19:21)*

Jesus really meant it. But alas! He could not follow Jesus because the Spirit had not yet been given, so there was no enablement, even if he wanted to.

While we may castigate this man and feel sorry for him that he could not follow Jesus because he had great possessions, we must realize that none of the disciples could follow Him either. Following Jesus is an enablement of the power of the Spirit and not a decision of the will of man. No man can ever come to Jesus except the Father draws him. (Joh 6:44) This is grace, and all that man needed to appropriate it is to respond in faith.

At Jesus' arrest, all His disciples fled except Peter who delayed his fleeing until he had denied his Master three times more (Mat 26:34-75). At the crucifixion, all the disciples 'abandoned' Jesus and went back to their businesses (Joh 21:3). The reason was because as at that time, the Holy Spirit had not been given and so, no one could truly follow Him without the enabling power of the Spirit.

The disciples had to wait for the Holy Spirit to come at Pentecost. When the Spirit came, He replaced their fear with faith and boldness, and they were not only able to follow Him, but also declared him boldly as Lord even before Pilate and Caesar unto death.

Both Nicodemus and the young ruler could not come to the reality of Jesus' invitation. The spirit had not been given for Nicodemus to experience the spirit baptism and power was yet to be released for the young ruler to follow Jesus because it was not the dispensation of following a Person, it was the dispensation of following the law and the prophets.

The church is now in the dispensation of following a Person, Jesus. Every believer must desire to manifest the life of Christ through His Spirit in him or her.

Many still live the Christian life today believing that the Spirit baptism is not for today and that it was just a one-time experience at Pentecost to usher in the Spirit and that it is no longer relevant. I believe it is a deception of the devil to rob believers of their lawful inheritance in Christ. This error of doctrine has made the church to be impotent, not being able to demonstrate the same power that the early church demonstrated. If the power was not for today, Jesus would not say that greater works than He did we would do. The only way we can do "greater works" is by the Spirit. If the Holy Spirit manifestation is not for today, then are we saying that Jesus made a wrong statement? What are we going to do with the prophecy of prophet Joel:

> *And it shall come to pass afterward, that I will pour out my spirit upon all flesh; and your sons and your daughters shall prophesy, your old men shall dream dreams, your young men shall see visions: And also upon the servants and upon the handmaids in those days will I pour out my spirit. (Joe 2:27-29)*

Are we going to expunge it from the Bible, look away and pretend that the prophecy was fulfilled in Pentecost alone, even though he mention sons, daughters, old men, young men, servants, handmaids. Were these people present in Pentecost? The prophecy was clear that it refers to the last days as he mentioned "afterward." The word of God endures forever and it is the same yesterday, today and forever.

It is when a believer experiences the spirit baptism that his faith walk is secured in Christ. It is a "faith walk," treading the path you do not know and you cannot by yourself. You have to depend on the Holy Spirit to lead you. That is where the faith in the walk comes from. If the Holy Spirit never came into your heart, He cannot lead you.

The spirit baptism, therefore, is the spiritual reality of the water baptism and water baptism is the physical reality of the spirit baptism. Both are necessary for a believer for a normal faith walk with Jesus.

Sometimes I like to equate baptism with worship. Many times we equate singing worship songs as worship. Singing worship songs does not mean that we are worshipping God. But when we worship God, songs can flow from deep in our hearts as a spontaneous response to our spirit worshipping God. Water baptism is like singing worship songs. It does not mean that you are baptized in the spirit. But when you are baptized in the spirit, you know the importance of water baptism.

Which comes first in the two baptisms: the water or the spirit? In the book of Acts chapter 19, we see that:

> *While Peter yet spake these words, the Holy Ghost fell on all them which heard the word. And they of the circumcision which believed were astonished, as many as came with Peter, because that on the Gentiles also was poured out the gift of the Holy Ghost. For they heard them speak with tongues, and magnify God. Then answered Peter, Can any man forbid water, that these should not be baptized, which have received the Holy Ghost as well as we? And he commanded them to be baptized in the name of the Lord. Then prayed they him to tarry certain days. (Act 10:44-48)*

In chapter 9, we see almost the direct opposite:

> *When they heard this, they were baptized in the name of the Lord Jesus. And when Paul had laid his hands upon them, the Holy Ghost came on*

> *them; and they spake with tongues, and prophesied. And all the men were about twelve. (Act 19:5-7)*

From these passages, some people received the baptism of the Holy Spirit before water baptism and some received it after. The important thing is to receive it. The Lord works in a dynamic way. If these two baptisms are not received after a man believes, then there is no way he can be saved, because it is he that believes and is baptized that shall be saved. The words of Jesus to Nicodemus is then very relevant:

> *Except a man be born of water and of the Spirit, he cannot enter into the kingdom of God. (Joh 3:5)*

When the Spirit baptism is received, it confers on the believer ability to manifest the gifts of the spirit for the glory of God and for the purpose of ministry. These nine gifts of the spirit are listed in 1Cor 12

> *Now there are diversities of gifts, but the same Spirit. And there are differences of administrations, but the same Lord. And there are diversities of operations, but it is the same God, which worketh all in all. But the manifestation of the Spirit is given to every man to profit withal. For to one is given by the Spirit the word of wisdom; to another the word of knowledge by the same Spirit; To another faith by the same Spirit; to another the gifts of healing by the same Spirit; To another the working of miracles; to another prophecy; to another*

discerning of spirits; to another divers kinds of tongues; to another the interpretation of tongues: But all these worketh that one and the selfsame Spirit, dividing to every man severally as he will. For as the body is one, and hath many members, and all the members of that one body, being many, are one body: so also is Christ.
(1Co 12:4-12)

Bern Zumpano makes a division of these gifts of the Spirit as follows:

A. REVELATION Gifts:
  1. *Gift of word of knowledge*
  2. *Gift of word of wisdom*
  3. *Gift of discernment of spirits*

B. 3 POWER Gifts:
  1. *Gift of faith*
  2. *Gift of miracles*
  3. *Gift of healings*

C. 3 VOCAL Gifts:
  1. *Gift of prophecy*
  2. *Gift of tongues*
  3. *Gift of interpretation of tongues* [ix]

These gifts will make believers not only to have an extra ordinary walk with Jesus but also a walk spiced with manifestation and demonstrations of the power of God. As we desire to walk with Him, let us avail ourselves of all the benefits attached to this promise. The gifts are for us.

> *Now we have received, not the spirit of the world, but the spirit which is of God; that we might know the things that are freely given to us of God. Which things also we speak, not in the words which man's wisdom teacheth, but which the Holy Ghost teacheth; comparing spiritual things with spiritual. (1Co 2:12-13)*

9

LIFE

"As ye have therefore received Christ Jesus the Lord, so walk ye in him."
- **Colossians 2:6**

Cry of Repentance

WHEN A BABY is born, there is something spectacular that everyone looks for in the wonderful event. It is the main event that determines if a life is birthed or not. When this event is absent, there is no joy even though a birth has occurred. It is the cry of the baby. If the baby does not cry, the midwives usually give a gentle spanking. This is to *awake* the baby and ensure that it is alive. Life is confirmed as the baby makes its first cry. It's a precious cry, the type that every mother looks forward to. It's the signal of life, people rejoice.

There is joy in heaven too when a soul is born into the kingdom and makes its first cry. If there is no cry, it means the birth did not lead to life: it is a stillbirth.

Do some births occur in the spirit without the initial cry of the baby? Does that mean that there is stillbirth even in the spirit? The answer to both questions is "yes."

Let us critically look at the words of Jesus again about the joy in heaven over a new birth:

> *I say unto you, that likewise joy shall be in heaven over one sinner that repenteth, more than over ninety and nine just persons, which need no repentance. (Luk 15:7)*

The key word in this verse is "one sinner that repents." Today, we have many sinners who come to Christ but there is no joy in heaven over it. This is because although birth did occur but there is no life in the birth, there is no initial cry that signifies life.

When the baby transforms from the life in the womb to the life in the world, the baby is conscious that there is a change of environment. There is an innate consciousness that it's another life. The body naturally responds to that in a cry.

The spiritual meaning of the cry is repentance. When there is a genuine repentance, there will be life, but when there is a birth without a cry (repentance) there is no life.

When a sinner is changed from within, there is a corresponding change from without. When a sinner is changed from a life of sin to a life of righteousness, there is a conviction, and a knowing inside that something has changed, from the old to the new. "If any man be in Christ, he is a new creature, old things a are passed away and all things are become new" (2Co 5:17).

The cry (of repentance) is the door to life. When Zacchaeus met with Jesus, there was a cry in him:

> *And Zacchaeus stood, and said unto the Lord; Behold, Lord, the half of my goods I give to the poor; and if I have taken any thing from any man by false accusation, I restore him fourfold. (Luk 19:8)*

If there is no repentance from the heart (a knowledge of a change), the mouth cannot cry. One person with a cry of repentance is better than ninety nine "just persons, which need no repentance." (Luk 15:7) The latter is often the rule today: people come to the Christian faith walk through a just means and not through the cry of repentance. Repentance is the beginning of a true spiritual journey.

After the cry of the baby, the rejoicing should not stop there. We cannot leave the baby to scavenge for survival on its own. The baby needs care, affection, and attention. While there is a great emphasis on birthing new souls into the kingdom, the life that follows should receive no less attention and emphasis. Conversion without discipleship leaves new converts stranded and crippled, unable to know how to walk. If truly there is a life, there must be a corresponding nurturing of that life till the baby learns how to sit, walk, talk and mature. Paul told the church at Collosse:

> *As ye have therefore received Christ Jesus the Lord, so walk ye in him: Rooted and built up in him, and*

stablished in the faith, as ye have been taught, abounding therein with thanksgiving. (Col 2:6-7)

The following seven actions are apparent in the scripture verses above.

1. RECEIVE Him
2. WALK with Him
3. ROOTED in Him
4. BUILT UP in Him
5. ESTABLISHED In Him
6. TAUGHT in Him
7. ABOUNDING in Him

Receive Him

Several times in the scripture we come across the word 'receive Christ.' This is the same as coming to Christ or the new birth. This is where you see Christ as not only a good man, a great prophet, a heroic figure, or an historic personality but the Savior of the world. Your heart of understanding is suddenly opened to see His glory. You see Him as The Way, the Truth and Life and that no one goes to the Father except by Him.

Many a new believer has no knowledge of what to do in Christ. Some are introduced to doing 'church.' They are committed to the set-man, being a part of the ministry, attend services regularly, join a department, go out regularly to evangelize in order to grow membership, give money for missions, enroll into the seminary to know more about the bible and possibly become ordained into an office in the denomination and so on. To the new believer, that is what it means to be a Christian. He grows in this and also initiates others coming after him into the same thing. So, the cycle continues to many generations, of believers who sincerely do not know what it is to come to Christ. Such cannot experience the life of Christ.

So, it is possible for a new believer to hobble in the same cycle of birth experience for the rest of his life without going further to explore other experiences. He may never know how to walk with Jesus, let alone how to mature in Him.

Receiving Christ or coming to Him confers on the believer the power and ability to become His son.

> *As many as received him, to them gave he power to become the sons of God, even to them that believe on his name: Which were born, not of blood, nor of the will of the flesh, nor of the will of man, but of God. (Joh 1:12-13)*

To become His son or daughter means to obey Him, to follow Him. It is in this process that the believer learns to be like Him. This process brings relationship, intimacy, and fruition. It brings love, worship, adoration and heart-knowledge of God, not head or lip knowledge.

Walk with Him

Walking with Christ however, is a step further from coming to Christ. Jesus does not want us to just come to Him and stay on the same spot, only relishing the experience. He bid us to walk with Him. The time we spend with Him when we initially come to Him is to sufficiently prepare us to walk with Him.

When Saul met and received Christ on the way to Damascus, it was just the beginning of his journey with the Lord. He must proceed on to the next stage, which is walking with Him. This is Discipleship. This is where he would experience Christ in a fuller dimension than he just did with the encounter he had. It is the stage to knowing more the very God he was persecuting with such zeal as a Pharisee. Only Jesus Himself can bring him or any new believer into this stage. Jesus told him:

> *Arise, and go into the city, and it shall be told thee what thou must do. (Act 9:6)*

What to do
This critical point in a believer's life is where he either gets it right or misses it completely. Paul had no clue what the future held for him. He just *lost* his life and he must now follow Jesus all the way. This is the same with anyone who had a genuine encounter with Jesus. It is one and the same as losing one's life. From this time onward, it is Jesus leading and directing.

So, Jesus led Saul to a specific man in a specific city for specific assignment. You will also discover that the same God that told Saul to go to the city for WHAT TO DO also went ahead to speak to a man in the city ON WHAT TO DO with Saul (a specific instruction on Saul):

And there was a certain disciple at Damascus, named Ananias; and to him said the Lord in a vision, Ananias. And he said, Behold, I am here, Lord. And the Lord said unto him, Arise, and go into the street which is called Straight, and enquire in the house of Judas for one called Saul, of Tarsus: for, behold, he prayeth, And hath seen in a vision a man named Ananias coming in, and putting his hand on him, that he might receive his sight. Then Ananias answered, Lord, I have heard by many of this man, how much evil he hath done to thy saints at Jerusalem: And here he hath authority from the chief priests to bind all that call on thy name. But the Lord said unto him, Go thy way: for he is a chosen vessel unto me, to bear my name before the Gentiles, and kings, and the children of Israel: For I will shew him how great things he must suffer for my name's sake. (Act 9:10-16)

Saul did not know this man and never met him before. Jesus knows who He would lead you to in order to reveal more of Himself to you. It is not the same person for every new believer. You and I may come to Christ at the same time and at the same channel, but we may be led to different persons. Saul's destiny as a true believer lay in the hands of this stranger, as it were. Remember, the purpose is to know more of Jesus. To do this, you must know what to do.

It is a common saying that no man can give what he does not have. This stranger Saul was about to meet would only be able to give him as much as he himself had, no more. What if he had so little? That is the situation today. The available men for such a task as this are scarce. Some of these men themselves don't even know what to do because when they came to Christ themselves, they were not led into a specific 'tutoring or mentoring' (discipleship), this becomes a generational cycle: a situation whereby many new believers do not know what to do and so cannot experience the full cycle of the normal Christian life. They grow to become as weak as their "mentor."

So, we see that coming to Christ is the first step in the series of Christ's experience. It is important that we know this order, for us and for those who come to Christ through us. This requires the work of faithful men who would truly lead new believers on the right path after they come to Christ. Not lead them to their denominations, ministries or projects.

The reason why walking with Christ seems difficult to many is because of the spiritual blindness and ignorance of the "midwives." Many are not properly trained in the art of midwifery. Some are just delivery assistants who never graduated or certified by the authorities. They became "midwives" by ideas, trial, and errors. More babies are lost rather than saved during the delivery process because of their incompetence. The pre-natal tests, instructions, and evaluations are not carried out to ensure that the baby is in proper position and ready for birth. During complex delivery process, the baby is lost. Those who survive are not given ideal post-natal care.

If you have truly received Him, then walk in Him. This is the place of abiding in Christ, the secret of believer's life and power.

As you can see, God always work with a witness. When He leads a man to someone, He tells the person about it. When He leads a new believer to an older believer for the purpose of leading him to a further walk with Christ, (not himself - discipleship), He also prepares the *discipler* to receive the disciple.

Discipleship

Let us examine Cornelius' encounter with Christ:

> *And when he looked on him, he was afraid, and said, What is it, Lord? And he said unto him, Thy prayers and thine alms are come up for a memorial before God. And now send men to Joppa, and call for one Simon, whose surname is Peter: He lodgeth with one Simon a tanner, whose house is by the sea side: he shall tell thee what thou oughtest to do. (Act 10:4-6)*

God did with Cornelius and Peter, what He did with Saul and Ananias. He will do the same with every believer. It is the heart of His relationship, it is discipleship. You must have the same experience. Paul led many new believers into the same experience in Christ. He said to the believers in the Corinthian Church:

> *For though ye have ten thousand instructors in Christ, yet have ye not many fathers: for in Christ Jesus I have begotten you through the gospel. (1Co 4:15)*

What a remarkable statement! Wished you could say that too. He also told Timothy, one of the people he personally brought up in the Lord:

> *The things that thou hast heard of me among many witnesses, the same commit thou to faithful men, who shall be able to teach others also. (2Ti 2:2)*

If God does not lead the new believer into this experience, He will be taken advantage of and led astray by those who claim to lead him into walk with God. Most of the time, they lead such new believer into membership of their ministry. Except God specifically lead believer to a specifically ordained disciple, he will be commercially institutionalized into a mere religious structure of man and not into Christ. It has to be God:

> *For it is God which worketh in you both to will and to do of his good pleasure. (Php 2:13)*

The truth is that today, personal discipleship has been substituted with institutional or system training. This does not bring relationship or life. That is why God did not give us a system, He gave us a Person, His Son, Jesus the Christ. Jesus desires a one to one relationship with us, not a general or formal training.

Sadly, there are institutions established that have taken over the task of discipling new believers. It is no longer a spiritual process but a religious program. It is at best initiation into individual pet projects. Remember, God always leads men to individuals who lead them to the fellowship, but never to an institution.

The new believer must get personal and intimate with God in order to hear this direction from God, otherwise, he will run to man. The man in turn will give him assignment of what to do in his own religious empire that he is building purportedly for God. To stabilize him more, he may gratify his ego by giving him a title on the guise of serving God or building a ministry for God. We can see this all around us today. God is neither building a ministry nor coming for a ministry: He is building His church and the church is men and women, not buildings, movement or denominations with its glorified institutions and empires.

The Voice of Eli

The calling or initiation of Samuel into the priesthood is a handy example of this. He got the call from God but being a 'new believer' as it were, or being naïve of the operations of God (it was his first encounter with God), he went to Eli, the prophet. He thought that the voice he heard was the voice of the prophet Eli whom he was growing familiar with. Eli was godly enough to tell Samuel WHAT TO DO. He did not lead Samuel to himself like many would do today: he led him back to God who called him. Only if leaders today would do this and not just give the new believer assignment in their organization!

Immediately we receive Him (come to Him), He gives us 'power to become.' This is the life of Christ in a believer. It is always at the instance of Christ, just like coming to Him is also at His instance. This is the (faith) walk with Jesus, discipleship. The power to become is the ability and divine enablement to walk with Him. As we do this, He builds our spiritual stamina.

Above the Law

Most fellowships today give laws, doctrines and so on as guidelines to follow. Good as these may be, it must not replace the voice of Jesus in a believer's life. Laws or doctrines cannot disciple people. They cannot give life. "…the letter (law) killeth, but the spirit giveth life." This is the reason why the law was abolished. God gave the law to show man that he could not keep it. The best of it cannot lead man to God. That's why Jesus came and we must give Him the chance to do the leading from this time on.

Saul heard a voice on the way to Damascus. The voice convicted him and saved him. The voice led him to Ananias to disciple him. The same voice was with Him throughout. That is the anointing John talked about:

> *The anointing which ye have received of him abideth in you, and ye need not that any man teach you: but as the same anointing teacheth you of all things, and is truth, and is no lie, and even as it hath taught you, ye shall abide in him. (1Jo 2:27)*

It is the voice of Jesus in a believer's life, the still small voice, the Spirit of Truth. Do you have it? Jesus said:

> *Howbeit when he, the Spirit of truth, is come, he will guide you into all truth: for he shall not speak of himself; but whatsoever he shall hear, that shall he speak: and he will shew you things to come. (Jo 16:13)*

When this Spirit is present in a believer, He makes him operate at a higher level –above the law.

Being above the law does not mean we are too arrogant to keep the law, but rather, whether the law is present or not, a believer is led by a higher power that is above the law and he cannot even break the law since basically, "…the law is not made for a righteous man, but for the lawless and disobedient, for the ungodly and for sinners, for unholy and profane, for murderers of fathers and murderers of mothers, for manslayers…" (1Ti 1:9)

When believers have to be guided by laws all the time, it is an indication of the absence of the Holy Spirit in them. It's like putting a yoke on oxen in order to force them to do what is intended to do.

> *For as many as are led by the Spirit of God, they are the sons of God. (Rom 8:14)*

Being led by God, however, requires absolute trust (faith). We must follow Him even though we don't know where He leads us to, but we trust that He cannot lead us astray.

This must not in any way energize or create an idea in us that we do not need doctrines or laws. This would only lead us into lawlessness if the Spirit does not stand in place to lead us into the truth. It's either we are led by the law or by the Spirit. The former leads to death and the latter leads to life. Life must be chosen by faith.

As said, believers are essentially people above the law. Not because they are arrogant or too spiritual to obey the law, but because the standard of operation of the Spirit of God in them is far higher than that of the law.

For instance, the law of adultery is when a man and woman have intercourse outside of marriage. But the spiritual standard of adultery for the NT believer is when you look at a woman to lust after her, the adultery is as good as committed. (Mat 5:28) You can see that Christians are essentially people 'above the law.'

In law, you only bring ten percent to God as your tithe but the standard of the Spirit for the NT believer is to bring one hundred percent. You don't bring a part of your income, you bring yourself and that includes all your income (Rom. 12:1).

Similarly, in the law, you have certain rights, but not in the Spirit. The moment you come to Jesus, you sign your life out and lose your right to the direction of the Holy Spirit. From then onward, you are controlled BY the Spirit.

Forgiveness is limited in law but limitless in the Spirit (Mat 18:22). Divorce is possible in the law of Moses, but not in the law of the Spirit (Mat 19:8). In the law, you run from evil, but in the spirit, you run from the appearance of evil. It is those who are led by the Spirit (not by the law) that are the sons and daughters of God. (Rom 8:14)

Rigorous doctrines of external piety to give a self-righteous and religious satisfaction are good but only for those who do not have the Spirit in them, such live in the flesh. "For if ye live after the flesh, ye shall die: but if ye through the Spirit do mortify the deeds of the body, ye shall live." (Rom 8:13)

> *I say then, Walk in the Spirit, and ye shall not fulfill the lust of the flesh. For the flesh lusteth against the Spirit, and the Spirit against the flesh: and these are contrary the one to the other: so that ye cannot do the things that ye would. But if ye be led of the Spirit, ye are not under the law. (Gal 5:16-18)*

Those who are guided by denominational laws and sincere doctrines of men are comparable to a white-washed sepulcher. They will pass external assessment of man's righteousness in denomination or religious parlance, but may not meet up with the standard of the Spirit. As the inside of a *beautiful* tomb is full of rottenness and diseases, so they appear in the spirit. They that walk in the flesh (the law) and not after the Spirit cannot please God.

> *For they that are after the flesh do mind the things of the flesh; but they that are after the Spirit the things of the Spirit. For to be carnally minded is death; but to be spiritually minded is life and peace. (Rom 8:5-6)*

The supposed [Christian] life that many live is but a life of observance of laws from a leader, person, system, movement, denomination, institution, or a cause. This is done with all commitment and faithfulness. It is good as a religious service but can hardly pass as a spiritual service. It is what is described as "living after the flesh."

> *If ye live after the flesh, ye will die: but if ye through the Spirit do mortify the deeds of the body, ye will live. For as many as are led by the Spirit of God, they are the sons of God. (Rom 8:13-14)*

Follow Me
The ministry of Jesus requires a following. Consistently throughout the scripture, the invitation to all the disciples is "follow me." (Joh 1:37-51) It is in following that there is life. Again, this is discipleship, the core of our faith. Many have truly come but are basking in that euphoria for many years, pursuing activities and following institutional laws but neglecting a personal relationship with Jesus.

Jesus could have asked the young ruler to come to Him. But he had already come to Christ. Jesus told him:

> *One thing thou lackest... follow me. (Mar 10:21)*

When Jesus told him to follow Him, it did not flow with his mindset. He was looking for some more laws to follow, not a person. Today too, many are looking for some real hard rules to follow to justify religious belief. There is a membership spirit, a sense of religious togetherness and association, a cultic bonding from a theological conviction of affiliation. That is why today, the harder the denominational rules, the more convinced those looking for something to do are. Such people love it hard.

In our Christian journey, let us be sure that we truly come to Him and not to another Jesus, denomination, sect, organization or religious movement. After we ascertain that, only one thing is needful, only one thing we lack, and that is to follow Him. That is the ultimate. Stop looking for something to do to please Him. There is nothing you can do to please Him than to follow Him. If you have come to Him, be sure to receive power to follow Him. Many will not follow Jesus until they see some fireworks. Jesus says to such:

> *A wicked and adulterous generation seeketh after a sign; and there shall no sign be given unto it, but the sign of the prophet Jonas. (Mat 16:4)*

The reason why following Christ is dear is because it comes with a huge price. "Then said Jesus unto his disciples, If any man will come after me, let him deny himself, and take up his cross, and follow me." (Mat 16:24)

Jesus asked one man to come follow Him but he said he wanted to go bury his father. Jesus told him: "Follow me; and let the dead bury their dead." (Mat. 8:22) The irony of it is that earlier in the same chapter, "a certain scribe came, and said unto him, Master, I will follow thee whithersoever thou goest. And Jesus saith unto him, The foxes have holes, and the birds of the air have nests; but the Son of man hath not where to lay his head." (Mat 8:19-20). One was willing to follow Jesus, He discouraged him from following Him; another didn't want to follow Him but He compelled him to follow Him. This is because we cannot follow Jesus by our will, it is by His power and by His Spirit. He calls whoever He wills. Paul says in Rom. 9:16:

> *So then it is not of him that willeth, nor of him that runneth, but of God that sheweth mercy. (Rom 9:16)*

The other man that Jesus discouraged from following him was called a 'Scribe,' a religious person. Religious people or those who love to be led by rules and laws rather than faith can hardly follow Jesus. Following Him is by simplicity of faith not by the complexity of the law or theology. It is not an academic or ideological assent of pursuit. We cannot learn how to follow him in Bible School or Seminary. We cannot learn it in our so-called Believers' Classes. We can only learn it by His Spirit.

> *For what man knoweth the things of a man, save the spirit of man which is in him? Even so the things of God knoweth no man, but the Spirit of God. (1Co 2:11)*

It is the Spirit that quickens (gives life), the flesh profits nothing. Jesus read the riot act to anyone who wants to follow Him:

> *Think not that I am come to send peace on earth: I came not to send peace, but a sword. For I am come to set a man at variance against his father, and the daughter against her mother, and the daughter-in-law against her mother-in-law. And a man's foes shall be they of his own household. He that loveth father or mother more than me is*

> *not worthy of me: and he that loveth son or daughter more than me is not worthy of me. And he that taketh not his cross, and followeth after me, is not worthy of me. He that findeth his life shall lose it: and he that loseth his life for my sake shall find it. (Mat 10:34-39)*

It is good to really count the cost because following Him will cost you. To follow Him, we must leave the comfort of the boat and rise to the words of Jesus that bid Peter come on the water. We cannot look at the water around us, but the Jesus ahead of us. He is the author and the finisher of our faith.

Paul wrote to the Romans:

> *And be not conformed to this world: but be ye transformed by the renewing of your mind, that ye may prove what is that good, and acceptable, and perfect, will of God. (Rom 12:2)*

It is in walking with Him that our soul man, who is not immediately saved when our spirit man is saved, receives gradual transformation and renewal. Sanctification is an ongoing work of the Holy Spirit in a believer's life. Paul calls it a "good work" and said it will be completed in the day of Jesus Christ (death or rapture (Phi 1:6). It's a "good work" because it produces the fruits of the Spirit in believer's life. It also gives the believer a divine ability not to conform to this world or love the world but be transformed. It gives the mind of Christ.

This transformation in the believer's life through the work of the Holy Spirit brings him or her to the image and likeness of

Jesus. This is our passport to get to heaven, we must look like Him. (Rom 8:29, Col 3:10)

> *Beloved, now are we the sons of God, and it doth not yet appear what we shall be: but we know that, when he shall appear, we shall be like him; for we shall see him as he is. (1Jo 3:2)*

This is the life of a Christian, a (faith) walk with Jesus through the Holy Spirit in him.

The Restorer
When we believe and we are baptized (water and spirit), we receive the Holy Spirit who indwells us. This Spirit performs various ministries in our lives as believers. He is the Restorer. He restores the relationship between God and man, which was strained in the Garden of Eden at the fall of man. With the ministry of the Holy Spirit, man can once again enjoy communion, communication and fellowship with God as it used to be. God again speaks with man in the cool of the day and man can hear His voice again with joy and no longer with fear. This is the first work of the Holy Spirit in a believer's life and this is what it means to be born again of the Spirit.

The Quickener
The Holy Spirit is also the quickening Spirit. He 'makes alive' the written word, the scriptures (Logos) and turns it into the revealed word (Rhema) in our hearts so that it can profit us. He is also the inner witness in our hearts. He convicts the world of sin (Joh 16:8).

One of the ministries of Satan is to accuse believers before the Lord (Rev 12:10, Job 1). He also constantly engages believers in battle in the mind, challenging and accusing believer that he is not a child of God. But "the Spirit itself beareth witness with our spirit, that we are the children of God." (Rom 8:16)

When Jesus was crucified and buried in the tomb, the Spirit of God in Him quickened (raised) Him again from the dead. Paul said:

> *If the Spirit of him that raised up Jesus from the dead dwell in you, he that raised up Christ from the dead shall also quicken your mortal bodies by his Spirit that dwelleth in you. (Rom 8:11)*

Quickening also means to make ready. The Holy Spirit prepares and 'make ready' the spirit in a believer for the Rapture of the church. Without this, the believer will not be able to be 'caught up to meet the Lord in the air.' (1Th 4:17) This is a great ministry of the Holy Spirit and it is His last work on earth. After this, He leaves the earth and the world degenerate into unimaginable chaos and the Great Tribulation. Without the Spirit, we cannot be raptured. Jesus Himself said:

> *It is the spirit that quickeneth... (Joh 6:63)*

The Restrainer

The Holy Spirit also does the work of the Restrainer. That is His function right now on earth. He restrains evil on the earth, especially the Anti-Christ.

> *For the mystery of iniquity doth already work: only he who now letteth will let, until he be taken out of the way. (2Th 2:7)*

When the Holy Spirit is 'taken out,' evil and the anti-Christ are no longer restrained. They appear on the scene to unleash untold hardship on the people of the world.

The Seal

Paul also called the Holy Spirit the Seal.

> *And grieve not the holy Spirit of God, whereby ye are sealed unto the day of redemption. (Eph 4:30)*

This ministry is important because Satan is actively pursuing and going after believers just as he did in the Garden of Eden to destroy Adam and Eve. Jesus told Peter:

> *Simon, Simon, behold, Satan hath desired to have you, that he may sift you as wheat: But I have prayed for thee, that thy faith fail not: and when thou art converted, strengthen thy brethren. (Luk 22:31-32)*

If the Holy Spirit does not seal believers till the last days, Satan will attempt to leave not even a remnant for Christ:

> *Except those days should be shortened, there should no flesh be saved: but for the elect's sake those days shall be shortened. (Mat 24:22)*

It is not this dispensation of the Gentiles alone that is sealed, Jesus also seals elects in the dispensation of the law and also at the period of the Great Tribulation in the next dispensation:

> *And I heard the number of them which were sealed: and there were sealed an hundred and forty and four thousand of all the tribes of the children of Israel. (Rev 7:4)*
>
> *Now he which stablisheth us with you in Christ, and hath anointed us, is God; Who hath also sealed us, and given the earnest of the Spirit in our hearts. (2Co 1:21-22)*

Immunity

Being sealed by the Holy Spirit is pretty much the same as being immunized against viruses and diseases in the physical.

When a baby is born, it is customary to give the baby some sorts of immunizations, this is called "acquired immunity." This is to boost the natural immunity the baby already has from the womb and also from other sources like food, particularly breast milk. With the advancement of science and technology, acquired immunity has greatly improved natural immunity to reduce infant mortality. This is also applicable in the spirit: when we come to Christ, we have a sort of natural immunity that prevents the enemy from destroying us. The more we feed on the sincere milk of the word, the more we get, and we pass from death unto life. Peter encouraged new believers thus:

> *As newborn babes, desire the sincere milk of the word, that ye may grow thereby. (1Pe 2:2)*

But then, we need the acquired immunity. This is to sustain and strengthen the natural immunity. This is not living by milk again but by meat. This time comes as we walk with the Lord. The writer of Hebrews was disappointed with certain people, and he said to them:

> *For when for the time ye ought to be teachers, ye have need that one teach you again which be the first principles of the oracles of God; and are become such as have need of milk, and not of strong meat. For every one that useth milk is unskilful in the word of righteousness: for he is a babe. But strong meat belongeth to them that are of full age, even those who by reason of use have their senses exercised to discern both good and evil. (Heb 5:12-14)*

This is the Holy Spirit in a believer's life: He immunizes him against sin. John wrote:

> *Whosoever is born of God doth not commit sin; for his seed remaineth in him: and he cannot sin, because he is born of God. (1Jn 3:9)*

We are encouraged not to grieve the Holy Spirit who seals us until the day of redemption (Eph 4:30). Life in a believer is worthwhile when it takes and sustains him till the day of redemption. "We are made partakers of Christ, if we hold the beginning of our confidence stedfast unto the end." This is the life of a believer.

10

ABUNDANT LIFE

*"I am come that they might have life,
and that they might have it more abundantly."*
- **John 10:10**

Sons to Glory

GOD TRULY DESIRES many to come to Him, but He wants children to mature into sons, and not to remain as children. Only a son, not a child can be entrusted with his father's estate: a child will squander and lose it because he is a child.

> *For it was fitting that he, for whom and by whom all things exist, in bringing many sons to glory...*
> *(Heb 2:10)*

Sons here mean matured children, heirs to the throne of the kingdom. But as long as they remain children, they cannot ascend to their rightful place of authority. This is the reason why God is committed to bringing sons to glory.

We come to God as a child, but we must mature in Him to become sons. An immature child (of God) is nothing but a slave to the enemy and the adversary. Even though he has everything by right, he cannot exercise the right as long as he is a child.

While many have truly come to Christ as infants, they are yet to grow and mature to be able to walk with Him. Some are learning to walk, but still wobble and fall.

Jesus gave the *five-fold* ministry to the church in order to mature children to sons; to help children perfect their walk and become stable.

> *And he gave some, apostles; and some, prophets; and some, evangelists; and some, pastors and teachers; For the perfecting of the saints, for the work of the ministry, for the edifying of the body of Christ: Till we all come in the unity of the faith, and of the knowledge of the Son of God, unto a perfect man, unto the measure of the stature of the fullness of Christ: That we henceforth be no more children, tossed to and fro, and carried about with every wind of doctrine, by the sleight of men, and cunning craftiness, whereby they lie in wait to deceive. (Eph 4:11-14)*

The church must not only come to Christ but also into the fullness of the heart of Christ. God has committed this reality into the hands of brothers among brethren within each local assembly so that there will be supply to the whole body. It is "for the administration of this service not only supplieth the want of the saints, but is abundant also by many thanksgiving unto God." (2Co 9:12)

It is only when those called into this responsibility see it and do it as unto the Lord that there will be unity of the faith and there will be a supply according to the effectual working in the measure of every part and there will be increase of the body (Eph 4:16). She has enormous task to do. This is a huge assignment, and it is not an office, but a calling (Luk 19:13, 1Co 6:2).

We cannot afford to be children: we must be perfected. If truly the saints shall judge the world and even angels, we must be able to "judge the smallest matters," and "…things that pertain to this life" (1Co 6:2-3) These do not look like assignment for children. Jesus did not just come to give us life but also abundant life, a matured life (Joh 10:10).

> *Now I say that the heir, as long as he is a child, differeth nothing from a servant, though he be lord of all; But is under tutors and governors until the time appointed of the father. Even so we, when we were children, were in bondage under the elements of the world. (Gal 4:1-3)*

An immature son is a mere slave, under the powers and influence of principalities, powers, demons and other elemental forces of this world. The enemy can still afflict any Christian that does not mature in Christ or walk in full provision of the life of Jesus, which is abundant life. Even though he has access to the power of Jesus that can bind Satan and put him under his feet, he can still be tossed to and fro, bound, oppressed and even die at the hands of the elements of the world, although his spirit is preserved.

The abundant life is a life that every believer cannot negotiate. If you do not have abundant life here on earth how would you move on to eternal life in heaven? This life is the maturation of the believer. It is the foretaste of the life with God in the eternal. It is essential therefore that every believer who already has a life of a faith-walk with Him desire abundant life in Him.

Walking in Power
Abundant life is not only a life of walking with God in the spirit but also walking in power on earth. It is having dominion over the power of darkness and putting them in chains and fetters by the authority of Jesus. This is the life God wants us to live here on earth before we reign with Him in heaven. He does not just want us to walk with Him and make our life a fragrance of love and grace to people, but also to set the captives free and command principalities and powers in dark places on their knees. If you are living a holy life and yet you are not taking authority over all the works of darkness, you may be walking with God, but not walking in the fullness of His power: you are not pressing into the fullness of His provisions for us here on earth; power needs demonstration.

We are not just saved here and kept for the next available flight to heaven. We are not saved and kept inactive, waiting for the time we will die. That is unproductive and unprofitable to God. His power on earth must be demonstrated through us. We are saved to show forth the life that God originally intended for the earth; the life Satan scuttled in the Garden. Otherwise, Jesus could have taken us into glory immediately we become born again. But He kept us so that we can live a victorious life through our godly character and demonstration of His power. By this, we become the epistle for the world (2Cor. 3:3), and we also tell the world that truly God has conquered the world and Satan has lost the battle.

Peter said:

> *Ye are a chosen generation, a royal priesthood, an holy nation, a peculiar people; that ye should shew forth the praises of him who hath called you out of darkness into his marvelous light: Which in time past were not a people, but are now the people of God: which had not obtained mercy, but now have obtained mercy. (1Pe 2:9-10)*

We must show the world that we have been called out of darkness into God's marvelous light. This will provoke the world to know that there is a generation of people who have conquered sin, sickness, and Satan.

Jesus gave the disciples a foretaste of this life while He was physically on earth with them. He gave them the power to heal and to bind devils.

> *And the seventy returned again with joy, saying, Lord, even the devils are subject unto us through thy name. And he said unto them, I beheld Satan as lightning fall from heaven. Behold, I give unto*

> *you power to tread on serpents and scorpions, and over all the power of the enemy: and nothing shall by any means hurt you. (Luk 10:17-19)*

It is not only living a life above sin but walking and demonstrating the power of God through the manifestations of the gifts of the Holy Spirit. We are to live a life of authority in the name of Jesus, subjecting Satan and all his cohorts under us. We are to take authority over demons, sicknesses, agents and agencies of the devil. We are to use the power to bind them and cast them out like Jesus did. This is walking in power: to heal the sick, mend the broken hearted and tell the oppressed that deliverance has come. This is the power that defies all the laws of darkness and brings the Shekinah glory and presence of God. This is the greatest defeat the devil can bear, and he will do everything and anything he can to try to prevent you from entering into it, including disbelief, fear or doubt. But you must press in into this life: it is the plan of God for every believer. God already made provision for you to come into it and have both the experience and manifestation of His power.

Jesus told the disciples:

> *Behold, I give unto you power to tread on serpents and scorpions, and over all the power of the enemy: and nothing shall by any means hurt you. (Luk 10:19)*
>
> *And these signs shall follow them that believe; In my name shall they cast out devils; they shall speak with new tongues; They shall take up*

> *serpents; and if they drink any deadly thing, it shall not hurt them; they shall lay hands on the sick, and they shall recover. (Mar 16:17-18)*

We see the experience and the manifestation of this authority in the life of the disciples. A poisonous snake wrapped around Paul's hand on the Island of Malta:

> *And when Paul had gathered a bundle of sticks, and laid them on the fire, there came a viper out of the heat, and fastened on his hand. And when the barbarians saw the venomous beast hang on his hand, they said among themselves, No doubt this man is a murderer, whom, though he hath escaped the sea, yet vengeance suffereth not to live. And he shook off the beast into the fire, and felt no harm. (Act 28:3-5)*

We cannot shake off the beast into the fire if we do not walk in power.

God desires us to replicate His authority on the earth as His sons and daughters. As long as we do this, we enforce His kingdom on earth and He is glorified. What a love!

> *Behold, what manner of love the Father hath bestowed upon us, that we should be called the sons of God: therefore the world knoweth us not, because it knew him not. Beloved, now are we the sons of God, and it doth not yet appear what we shall be: but we know that, when he shall appear, we shall be like him; for we shall see him as he is.*

> *And every man that hath this hope in him purifieth himself, even as he is pure. (1Jo 3:1-3)*
>
> *We are the children of promise not that of the bondwoman. God is expecting us, one day, to take our rightful place in the eternal scheme of things. (1Co 6:3)*

It's a Relationship
Abundant life is a life of both inward and outward relationships. The inward relationship is having personal fellowship with God and with the brethren, the outward relationship is manifesting the love of God to those who are lost through outreach.

Mission is generally called the heartbeat of God. The command of Jesus for outreach is also generally called The Great Commission:

> *Go ye therefore, and teach all nations, baptizing them in the name of the Father, and of the Son, and of the Holy Ghost: Teaching them to observe all things whatsoever I have commanded you: and, lo, I am with you alway, even unto the end of the world. Amen. (Mat 28:19-20)*

These require inward and outward relationships, which is sadly but fast becoming extinct in the last day church.

We really cannot do one and leave the other. We cannot be too spiritual: having personal fellowship with God and the brethren, yet neglect to reach the lost. We also cannot be too zealous for God, organizing crusades, involved in evangelism and mission for the lost and forgetting to have fellowship with brethren. This relationship is a cycle: one feeds the other and one is not complete without the other. We receive life when we have fellowship with God and with the brethren. This life is for our personal growth. It is also to receive spiritual strength and stamina to go out to the lost. We bring the lost into the fellowship to experience the relationship with God and with other brethren. After a while, they also develop to repeat the cycle.

Many are at ease with their salvation (Amo 6:1). They are truly having fellowship with God and with the brethren but are deficient in the area of outreach. It is a reflection of not fully pressing in into the fullness of Christ. It is not walking in the full provision of God for believers; it is not walking in the abundant life.

The Great Commission is the demonstration of the life we receive in fellowship. It is expressed outside, not inside. God has designed it so. It is the overflow of His life in us. When we are all full in the fellowship and there is no way to channel our overflow, we will begin to bite one another.

> *But if ye bite and devour one another, take heed that ye be not consumed one of another. (Gal 5:15)*

A dam receives and receives, but if there is no channel to discharge what it receives, it starts to stink. The only treatment to prevent stench among the brethren is to release the abundance of what God has poured into us, it is to demonstrate the life that you have received in the fellowship out where the sinners are. When sinners are saved and brought to the fellowship, it reignites the power and presence of God within the fellowship, otherwise, the local assembly becomes doctrinal, judgmental, faultfinding and frustrated bunch of people.

When we plug into this cycle, we become fruitful unto the Lord. We become like a tree that bears fruit for the Master and ready to receive the blessing attached to this:

> *Every branch in me that beareth not fruit he taketh away: and every branch that beareth fruit, he purgeth it, that it may bring forth more fruit. (Joh 15:2)*

This is what you and I have been called to do.

Rejoice in your salvation, but also have the mind of Christ for the lost: He saves you and expects you to go tell the good news of how His power saved you, and that the same power can save them. He desires all men to come to Him. Jesus died for all. He wants those who are already with Him to go to those who are not yet. But if you are too religious with your salvation, how will He reach them? If everybody does what you do, not wanting to reach out, how would you have ever come to Him? You are saved to save others, not by your power, effort or zeal but by simply telling them of the grace that saved you. When we ask the Lord to lead us to who He wills, He will do that because only Him can bring people to Himself; we are just His channel and we must move by His leading and direction

Fire Baptism

In the previous chapters, we examined what the writer of the book of Hebrews in chapter six and verse one call the "basic principles of the doctrines of Christ. We have treated each of the steps highlighted in this verse. The first step, which is repentance from dead works, the second is faith towards God, and the third, baptisms.

In the doctrines of baptisms, we pointed out that a new believer needs two baptisms: water and spirit baptisms. However, there is yet another baptism, *fire baptism*. This is the completion of the cycle of baptism for a normal Christian growth. This baptism only occurs in the cycle of abundant life of a believer.

Many think that fire baptism is the same as spirit baptism. The major reason is because it says in the book of Acts:

> *And when the day of Pentecost was fully come, they were all with one accord in one place. And suddenly there came a sound from heaven as of a rushing mighty wind, and it filled all the house where they were sitting. And there appeared unto them cloven tongues like as of fire, and it sat upon each of them. And they were all filled with the Holy Ghost, and began to speak with other tongues, as the Spirit gave them utterance. (Act 2:1-4)*

Many interpret the phrase "cloven tongues as of fire" as fire baptism that the apostles experienced at this scene. But this was only a description of the utterance of the people. This is buttressed by the fact that it says, "like as of fire." It is not fire itself, but so it looked to them. It is one and the same as when somebody speaks as if coals of fire were in his mouth making his tongue to run fast.

The mother of the Zebedees came to Jesus and requested that He grant the two of her children to sit one on his left side and the other on the right side in the kingdom.

> *But Jesus answered and said, Ye know not what ye ask. Are ye able to drink of the cup that I shall drink of, and to be baptized with the baptism that I am baptized with? They said unto him, we are able. (Mat 20:22)*

Jesus here was speaking of a baptism other than water and Spirit baptisms. We can recall that He already passed through both. He was talking of a baptism that was in view: "...the cup that I shall drink and to be baptized with the baptism that I am baptized with." This is fire baptism.

He first answered the Zebedees that they didn't know what they were asking for. If they knew, they wouldn't dare ask for it. Nobody who truly knows what this is would actually ask for it. Indeed they didn't know what they were asking for. James was the first to be beheaded in accordance with their request, and John passed through many ordeals as a living witness.

According to Bern Zumpano:

> *Fire baptism is ...immersion into the afflictions, sufferings, trials, oppositions and tribulations of life which try, test, and build our faith. In*

> *scriptures, these are known as "valley experience" and our "walk through "the valley of the shadow of death." (Psa 23) Our faithwalk is built up through these experiences and the Lord trains us in patience, endurance, holiness, righteousness and teaches is to walk in VICTORY. And so the scriptures states that by these we go "from faith to faith..." that is, from one test of faith to ever increasing step of faith, and from "glory to glory..." that is, from victory to victory. God assures us of victory each time... FOR HIS GLORY, until He brings us to that place of SPIRITUAL MATURITY where we need to be. Then, the trials and tribulations CEASE and He establishes us.*
>
> *...The FIRE BAPTISM WILL COME upon the life of every believer as a SOVEREIGN WORK OF GOD specific for His purpose and His plan for the believer's life. The believer's response MUST be to YIELD, TRUST and walk by FAITH.* [x]

God uses the fire baptism to purge believers so that he can 'bring forth more fruit." The purging of the believer requires pruning, cutting, straightening and so on. This doesn't come as easy as it sounds for the believer. It is indeed a baptism, a dunking under and total immersion into the suffering of Christ. Zumpano says further:

> *The New Testament word for "fire" is the Greek word "pur", literally meaning both "fire" and*

> *"lightening." It is not only a symbol of the Holy Spirit and of God's judgment, but in the New Testament "fire" scriptures, it specifically speaks of that which TRIES THE FAITH of the believer, producing in them the FRUITS of the Spirit (Gal 5:22,23), and glorifying the Lord. It is symbolic of the TRIALS, TRIBULATIONS, OPPOSITIONS, PERSECUTIONS and AFFLIC-TIONS that ALL Christians MUST suffer in order to make them conform to the IMAGE and LIKENESS of Christ, the PROCESS being their PERFECTION, that is, their being brought into SPIRITUAL MATURITY.* [xi]

The only school God sends His children to is the school of affliction and suffering. This is not because He hates them but because He must wean and prune them of every dross, dirt and the tiniest speck. They must have the same testimony like Jesus: "… for the prince of this world cometh, and hath nothing in me." (John 14:30) This is only achieved by fire. It may look like suffering to us but it is the price that we have to pay to mature in Him. He paid the same price and we must be like Him and to look like him and conform to His image. Only then can we say:

> *Beloved, now are we the sons of God, and it doth not yet appear what we shall be: but we know that, when he shall appear, we shall be like him; for we shall see him as he is. (1Jo 3:2)*

When we pass through this stage, we do not bemoan our situation but we rejoice in Him, that we are made to be partaker, not only of His life, but also His death. When the disciples passed through this stage, they rejoiced "and they departed from the presence of the council, rejoicing that they were counted worthy to suffer shame for his name." (Act 5:41)

> *But rejoice, inasmuch as ye are partakers of Christ's sufferings; that, when his glory shall be revealed, ye may be glad also with exceeding joy. (1Pe 4:13)*
>
> *Wherefore let them that suffer according to the will of God commit the keeping of their souls to him in well doing, as unto a faithful Creator. (1Pe 4:19)*
>
> *If we suffer, we shall also reign with him: if we deny him, he also will deny us. (2Ti 2:12)*

Jesus endured because of the glory that was set before Him, we must also endure for the sake of the glory that Jesus has called us into. It is an eternal glory, which transcends any earthly experience.

> *But the God of all grace, who hath called us unto his eternal glory by Christ Jesus, after that ye have suffered a while, make you perfect, stablish, strengthen, settle you. (1Pe 5:10)*

We cannot get there if we do not allow Him to remove in us all that cannot pass on into this glory. We must look up to Him, not the suffering. Paul said:

> *For I consider that the sufferings of this present time are not worth comparing with the glory that is to be revealed to us. (Rom 8:18)*
>
> *Looking unto Jesus the author and finisher of our faith; who for the joy that was set before him endured the cross, despising the shame, and is set down at the right hand of the throne of God. (Heb 12:2)*

We have in our bodies the mark of Christ.

> *For as the sufferings of Christ abound in us, so our consolation also aboundeth by Christ. (2Co 1:5)*

Despite the high stake of maturing in Christ, we must desire maturity, because it is the fullness of the born again experience of a believer and does not come cheap.

> *For it became him, for whom are all things, and by whom are all things, in bringing many sons unto glory, to make the captain of their salvation perfect through sufferings. (Heb 2:10)*

Signs of Abundant Life

The normal cycle of the natural man is to be born, to live and to die. The normal cycle of the spiritual man is to be born (again), to have life (in Christ) and to have abundant life (in God). While death is the end of life for the natural man, abundant life is just the beginning of another life for the spiritual man. If you want eternal life, go for abundant life here on earth, it is the foretaste of eternal life in heaven.

While many are still groping with having the life of Christ, which is the (faith) walk with Christ, abundant life (maturity in Christ) seems like something far away. You must come to terms with the fact that the minimum God designs and expects from you is abundant life. It has a steep price but the benefit far outweighs the price. Aside from the fact that it is the door to eternal life, it is the life designed for us by God.

The disciples of Jesus suddenly came to the realization of the cost of following Jesus. This was precedented by the decision of the rich young ruler who could not pay the price. Jesus watched the man left, He did not call him back. What really amazed the disciples was when Jesus said, "how hard is it for them that trust in riches to enter into the kingdom of God! It is easier for a camel to go through the eye of a needle, than for a rich man to enter into the kingdom of God. And they were astonished out of measure, saying among themselves, Who then can be saved?" (Mar 10:23-26)

Good question: "who then can be saved?"

The rich man is not the usual day-to-day regular man, no, not in Israel. Rich, young, ruling, and love the Lord! Yet he could not meet the requirement. Right there and then the disciples knew they were outrightly disqualified. Peter quickly said, "lo, we have left all, and have followed thee." (Mar 10:28)

The answer of Jesus is very comforting:

> *Verily I say unto you, There is no man that hath left house, or brethren, or sisters, or father, or mother, or wife, or children, or lands, for my sake, and the gospel's, But he shall receive an hundredfold now in this time, houses, and*

> brethren, and sisters, and mothers, and children, and lands, with persecutions; and in the world to come eternal life. But many that are first shall be last; and the last first. (Mar 10:28-31)

We can see here that even though it is hard for the rich to enter the kingdom of heaven and also easier for a camel to go through the eye of a needle, than for a rich man to enter into the kingdom of God, yet there is a material blessing for believers who follow Him. Following God does not mean poverty or penury. We must have a healthy view about this. It is not a sin to be rich, but it is God that brings the riches for His glory.

When Jesus said:

> How hardly shall they that have riches enter into the kingdom of God! And the disciples were astonished at his words. But Jesus answereth again, and saith unto them, Children, how hard is it for them that trust in riches to enter into the kingdom of God. (Mar 10:23)

They that trust in riches! Paul also said:

> But they that will be rich fall into temptation and a snare, and into many foolish and hurtful lusts, which drown men in destruction and perdition. (1Ti 6:9)

They that will be rich...

> But those who desire to be rich. (ESV).
>
> They that are minded to be rich. (ASV)

Those with an inordinate desire or excessive desire to be rich. But there is another riches:

> *The blessing of the LORD, it maketh rich, and he addeth no sorrow with it. (Pro 10:22)*

Paul went further to say:

> *For the love of money is the root of all evil: which while some have coveted, they have erred from the faith, and pierced themselves through with many sorrows. (1Ti 6:10)*

The desire and the love of money lead many into diverse lusts and temptation.

> *But every man is tempted, when he is drawn away by his own lust, and enticed. Then when lust hath conceived, it bringeth forth sin: and sin, when it is finished, bringeth forth death. (Jas 1:14-15)*

The point here is that there are blessings and riches that is from that Lord. When Peter said that "Lo, we have left all, and have followed thee." Jesus said they would receive "an hundredfold now in this time, houses, and brethren, and sisters, and mothers, and children, and lands, with persecutions; and in the world to come eternal life." (Mat 10:29)

Do not forget that the riches and blessings are only for those who are living the abundant life. The riches are released in trust to them for the sake of the kingdom. This is because the kingdom of God comes with both power and authority.

It is released to those who have no desire for money or the love of the money. They are trustees. How God needs people like this. He wants to entrust the riches of the kingdom into many hands but He is *afraid* of losing them. Many are only close to God in times of need. That is why these riches and gifts come "with persecution..."a somewhat *thorn in the flesh.*

For every gift of God released to His children, He guides it jealously in them so that the gifts do not control them or replace Him in their lives. God always give grace before releasing the glory (Psa 84:11), otherwise, the glory will kill. Paul said:

> *And lest I should be exalted above measure through the abundance of the revelations, there was given to me a thorn in the flesh, the messenger of Satan to buffet me, lest I should be exalted above measure. For this thing I besought the Lord thrice, that it might depart from me. And he said to me, My grace is sufficient for thee: for my strength is made perfect in weakness. Most gladly therefore will I rather glory in my infirmities, that the power of Christ may rest upon me. (2Co 12:7-9)*

The perfection of the gift of God is released with a weakness in man. This is so that man will not glory in himself or usurp the glory of God. So that he will know that it is not him doing it but God in him, and without the God in him, he is absolutely nothing. We cannot pray this away because it is put there by God to buffet us, to keep us under and humble us. As Paul said: so that due to the abundance of revelation, he will not be puffed up. This is a possibility as long as we are in this coat of flesh.

If you read further in the passage where Jesus assured the disciples about their reward in following Him, He said: "a hundredfold now in this time, houses, and brethren, and sisters, and mothers, and children, and lands…"

From Death to Abundant Life
One of the most remarkable points about this last stage in the Normal Christian Cycle is the substitution power in this stage. According to the cycle of the natural man, it is Birth, Life and Death. But in the cycle of the spiritual man, it is Birth, Life and Abundant Life. Death has been substituted with Abundant Life. "O death, where is thy sting? O grave, where is thy victory?" (1Co 15:55) The truth is that death has been swallowed up in victory.

If you are afraid of death, it is perhaps an indication that you are not yet living in the abundant life of God. He who lives in abundant life of God already has the sentence of death in himself. So, death means nothing but the way to eternal life. (2Co 1:9) If you already have the sentence of death in yourself, how can you be afraid of death any longer? Paul said, "…for to me to live is Christ, and to die is gain." (Phi 1:21) The same must be applicable to us, too.

Many have denied their Lord and Master in the face of persecution and threat of death. Many have denied the faith and turned back. They have confessed other gods in order to escape death. Does this mean they do not possess the life of Christ? Does this mean they were never born into the kingdom and have the experience of a genuine faith walk with Christ? This is not necessarily the case. Judas had a faith walk with Christ. And there are many examples in the New Testament of those who denied the faith. Paul mentioned a couple of people. Denying this is to say that there is no backsliding.

The writer of the book of Hebrews opened the window on this topic:

> *For it is impossible for those who have been once enlightened, and have tasted the heavenly gift, and have been made partakers of the Holy Spirit. And have tasted the good word of God, and the powers of the world to come, If they shall fall away, to renew them again to repentance; seeing they crucify to themselves the Son of God afresh, and put him to an open shame. (Heb 6:4-6)*

This means that someone who has experienced the following:

- Once enlightened (born again)
- Tasted the heavenly gift
- Made partakers of the holy spirit
- Tasted the good word of God
- Tasted the powers of the world to come

can still "fall away." Not only is this possible but to redeem them is (almost) impossible.

If you study the verse carefully, the reason why it says it is impossible is because if they must return, they must be renewed "again to repentance." This means that they must start the process of the elementary principles of the doctrines of Christ all over again. According to Hebrews chapter six, this begins with repentance from dead works, then faith towards God...

The possibility of a believer to draw back (backslide) is also highlighted in the words of Paul to the Thessalonians:

> *Let no man deceive you by any means: for that day shall not come, except there come a falling away first, and that man of sin be revealed, the son of perdition... (2Th 2:3)*

There must be a falling away of those who are already standing. Only someone who stands can fall, and this is a characteristic of the last day believer... "the day shall not come..." the final day, the rapture of the church shall not occur until many who are standing fall.

> *Now the Spirit speaketh expressly, that in the latter times some shall depart from the faith, giving heed to seducing spirits, and doctrines of devils. (1Ti 4:1)*

> *For the time will come when they will not endure sound doctrine; but after their own lusts shall they heap to themselves teachers, having itching ears; And they shall turn away their ears from the truth, and shall be turned unto fables. (2Ti 4:3-4)*

While writing to the church at Collose, Paul mentioned someone by the name of Demas: "Luke, the beloved physician, and Demas, greet you." (Col 4:14) In his letter to the Phillipian Church, he called him "fellowlabourer." (Phm 1:24) But while writing to the Thessalonians, he said:

> *For Demas hath forsaken me, having loved this present world, and is departed unto Thessalonica... (2Ti 4:10)*

Peter also mentioned some "which have forsaken the right way, and are gone astray, following the way of Balaam the son of Bosor, who loved the wages of unrighteousness." (2Pe 2:15) This refers to those who are in the ministry for profit.

When such people fall, they have fallen from the spiritual man to the natural man and the power of death is activated in their lives once again. But he that endures to the end has conquered death till eternity.

Martyrs of Christ
There have been many reported cases of Christian persecutions around the world, especially in the Islamic dominated countries. In Northern Nigeria, Christians are daily slaughtered like chickens by Muslims who are acting on the mandate to *"completely eradicate in its entirety all forms of worship different from Islam including, especially but not limited to Christianity."*

There were reported cases of Muslims surrounding many Christian churches during worship service, locked the worshippers inside, poured gasoline in and around the building, then set the building on fire while they rejoice in the cry and scream of the people as they roast to death. The case of the Deeper Life Bible Church in Kaduna gained prominent attention in the news media including Wikipedia. Worshippers were sprayed with AK-47 bullets from the doors and windows. [xii]

In other strange development, it was reported that Christians were rounded up and lined up, and one by one, they were led to slaughter. They must either deny Christ and allowed to live or confess Christ and be killed. The latter were cruelly slaughtered by carpenter's saw, and thrown to a mass grave just beside.

The most amazing thing out of the report, which was reportedly recorded and circulated among believers in the southern part for the purpose of prayer, was that each of the believers who were lined up for the slaughter were made to watch how their fellow believers were being slaughtered and rolled into the grave. This was to instill fear in them so that they could deny Jesus. But rather for them to deny Jesus, they were rejoicing and singing. They did not wait to be called for the slaughter, each went willingly at his turn. Denying Christ was not an option. They lied down by themselves ready to die for whom they believed in. Only those who are living in abundant life can do this. To them, to die is gain.

Of a particular interest was a case of a brother in this group. The fear of death gripped him and he was reported to have denied Christ. But the twist to the story as told was that when he denied Christ, the commander who was the brain behind the massacre immediately jumped forward and offered to take his place. He commanded his men to slaughter him in place of the Christian brother who just denied Christ. It was thought to be a joke, but when the commander himself shot one of his own men dead for refusing to slaughter him, they became confused.

According to the story, he claimed that each time the Christians were slaughtered and the head severed from the body, while the body is rolled into the mass grave, he saw them rise again almost instantaneously, and their head returned to their necks, smiling with such peace and joy that he could not describe. He said further that they all had a golden crown on their head. This, he said happened to every single one that was slaughtered.

So, when one of the Christians denied Christ, he saw it as an opportunity to take his place so he could experience that and receive the golden crown. He thought it was real and everyone was seeing it, but God deliberately opened only his eyes to see. That was his own Damascus experience that led him to the same Lord he once persecuted. This is similar to the experience of Saul who later became Paul. Let us pray that God would use this man for his glory as He did Paul, and let us also pray for the family of those martyred for their faith, that God would console and comfort them, and that God will give the saints in this place boldness, and the gatherings will wax stronger in the midst of the continued persecution. The blood of the saints is the fertilizer that waters the seed of the gospel in these regions. Let us remember them as well as many saints who are persecuted in Iran, Iraq, Syria, Pakistan and other parts of the world in our prayers.

The Way to Life

These martyrs are true overcomers. They truly conquered death. To them, the second death has no power because "they loved not their lives unto the death." (Rev 12:11)

It is good to have life, but not sufficient to stay at that spot. It is better to have abundant life. Jesus said:

> *I have come that you may have life and have it more abundantly. (Joh 10:10)*

Jesus was able to lay down his life because He already defeated death, same with His disciples. Stephen was described as a man full of faith and Holy Ghost. He did not see death, even though his killers surrounded him. He saw the "heavens opened and the Son of man standing on the right hand of God." (Act 7:56) He was able to pray for his killers. Death was a means to eternal life to Him. He was already operating in abundant life.

The Bible may not give us the detailed account of how all the disciples died. But traditions has it that almost all of them with the exception of John died as martyrs. According to the sources, Peter did not want to be equal with his Lord and Master in death, so he requested to be crucified upside down. It is obvious that he was not afraid of death. To such, death has lost its power. They had the sentence of death in themselves and have conquered death.

This explains the reason we wonder why God, many times, did not prevent his disciples or believers from death. Loss is painful to us in every form, but to God, it is a door to eternity. To many, it is the most permanent healing.

The only reason Paul wanted to live was because of the people, but personally, he wished to be with the Lord. Do you so wish? Do you panic in the face of death and run helter-skelter? It means you have more possession here on earth than in heaven, for where you treasure is, there your heart will be also. (Mat 6:21)

In his epistle to the Philippian church, Paul said:

> *For I am in a strait betwixt two, having a desire to depart, and to be with Christ; which is far better: Nevertheless to abide in the flesh is more needful for you. (Php 1:23-24)*

He also says that being in this body is a burden and he groans to leave it so that life can swallow it up. (2Co 5:4) Here is a man that was truly living in abundant life and all he was looking forward to was eternal life (1Co 15:53).

The question is: what will make a man desire to die if not for the hope that is ahead of him? He said to the Corinthian church:

> *If in this life only we have hope in Christ, we are of all men most miserable. (1Co 15:19)*

> *For we know that if our earthly house of this tabernacle were dissolved, we have a building of God, an house not made with hands, eternal in the heavens." (2Co 5:1)*

We must purify ourselves with this hope and death will mean nothing to us. (1Jn 3:3) If we live, it is for Christ, if we die, it is gain.

Indeed life is good, but the truth is that no matter how good and beautiful life is, we do not belong here. The best beauty of the earth is like a jungle to God. Our land of nativity is heaven. We are sojourners here on earth and we should not allow ourselves to be earth-bound.

God instructed Israel not to build any permanent structure on their way to the Promised Land, and also not to intermarry with the people they met on their way. They were to always watch the cloud when it moved, they must move with it. If they bought lands and married in a strange land, it would be difficult for them to move when the cloud moved. We must not be caught in this thicket.

When death is defeated in your heart, it has no power again in your life. Those who are yet to defeat death in their heart live in constant fear of death; they are slaves to death. When they drive, fly, sleep, fall sick or pass through any strange experience, fear of death is palpable. They die even before death kills them.

The early church was able to demonstrate the power and glory of God in signs, miracles, and spiritual growth because they experienced all, not just a part of the fullness of Christ. To them, it was not a program but a process. The Holy Spirit took them through normal Christian cycle. He would do the same for you and I if we are humble enough. This is when we can experience the power of God as it was in the early church.

Abundant life is the door to eternal life. God expects you and I to live this life as a precursor to the life to come. Are you ready to move up to this life?

OTHER BOOKS BY THE AUTHOR

- What God Forgot To Say
- Mystery of Union in Marriage
- Capsules of Faith

UPCOMING BOOKS

- The Companion Booklet to The Normal Christian Cycle.
- The Mystery of the Two Churches; The church that Jesus built and the church that Satan built.
- Spiritual Recipe: Five Ingredients of a Godly Marriage

The Great Possession

Riches and Wealth are Great Possessions, but there is a greater possession...
'Bola Olu-Jordan
Pages: 73, paperback
ISBN: 978978-5037715
Publisher: CRYOUT Publishing

When do riches, wealth or possessions become stumbling block to get to the kingdom of God and when do they become asset leading to the Kingdom? This book will help you discover this and how the most difficult things you could ever let go in your life can be a blessing, rather than a spiritual burden in your Christian journey.

REVIEWS

I have read many books on discipleship, but I was actually looking for something like a Jesus'-style discipleship: something practical, where Jesus was the discipler with other people aside from the twelve disciples. I found it in this book. I will recommend it to any believer who wants the "real meat" of the WORD.

Easy read. Enjoy the simplicity in sharing the treasure in being a disciple of Christ. Would recommend this to anyone who desires more knowledge on what it means by being a disciple.

The author captured the importance of discipleship in mentoring and teaching the body of Christ because this is what is lacking in the body. The tools giving in this book about discipleship will equip all believers in their walk with Christ.

I Know Your Works
Your eternity depends on the verdict of one Man and He has something against you!
'Bola Olu-Jordan
Pages: 84, paperback
ISBN: 978-9785037739
Publisher: CRYOUT Publishing

You are invited to the banquet of a Great King by one of His lords. You bring your best gift to honor the king. He likes the gift, but your name is not in the guest list. Only the prince can bring you in, but he wants something you don't have. When your works and labor are acceptable to God, what else could He be looking for? This book shows you what it is, and how you can have it. It is the only requirement to make heaven!

REVIEWS

This book tells the truth and will challenge you in your walk with the Lord. It tells exactly how we can know if we are where we should be in our relationship with God and how we can come to the place we need to be in order to please the Father and it is not by our good works. It is an easy to read book and I recommend it to others!

...Helping the body of Christ understand the process of discipleship through true relationship with Christ, and not just through works as we have been conditioned. The book will cut deep into the desires and intent of our heart to push us to introspect our self and our ways as believers of Christ. We must not only know His acts but also His ways and that is only birth through intimacy with the Christ. Overall, awesome read!

ABOUT THE AUTHOR

Bola Olu-Jordan grew up in Africa where much of his spiritual development was birthed. He pastored in a large denomination for several years and was actively involved in church planting, mission outreaches, discipleship and leadership trainings. He presently fellowships with a local gathering from where the Lord open doors of fellowship with brethren around the world. He is married and blessed with children.

Connect with the author:
www.facebook.com/bolabolujordan
www.twitter.com/ojordanist
CRYOUTPublishing.com/bola-olu-jordan.html

NOTES

NOTES

NOTES

REFERENCES

[i] Pawson, David. *The Normal Christian Birth.* (pp. 99) True Potential Publishing, SC, USA. 1989

[ii] Oxforddictionaries.com

[iii] Gordon Gentry, Ministry. (pp.7) New Testament Church Source. FL. USA. 2010

[iv] Pawson, David. *The Normal Christian Birth.* (pp. 41) True Potential Publishing, SC, USA. 1989

[v] Pawson, David. *The Normal Christian Birth.* (pp. 22-23) True Potential Publishing, SC, USA. 1989.

[vi] Pawson, David. *The Normal Christian Birth.* (pp. 23) True Potential Publishing, SC, USA. 1989.

[vii] Zumpano, Bern. *Bible Basics for Kingdom Living.* (pp. 43) Harbor Light Publishing. Miami, Florida. 1989

[viii] Pawson, David. *The Normal Christian Birth.* (pp. 12) True Potential Publishing, SC, USA. 1989.

[ix] Zumpano, Bern. *Bible Basics for Kingdom Living.* (pp. 47) Harbor Light Publishing. Miami, Florida. 1989

[x] Zumpano, Bern. *Bible Basics for Kingdom Living.* (pp. 244-245) Harbor Light Publishing. Miami, Florida. 1989

[xi] Zumpano, Bern. *Bible Basics for Kingdom Living.* (pp. 244) Harbor Light Publishing. Miami, Florida. 1989

[xii] *https://en.wikipedia.org/wiki/Deeper_Life_Church_shooting*

www.ingramcontent.com/pod-product-compliance
Lightning Source LLC
Chambersburg PA
CBHW031638040426
42453CB00006B/142